Black Dog Folklore

Mark Norman

Black Dog
FOLKLORE

Mark Norman

A comprehensive study of the image of the Black Dog
in folklore, with an extensive gazetteer of over 700 UK
sightings and traditions

TROY BOOKS

ISBN 978-1-909602-13-7

Published by Troy Books
www.troybooks.co.uk

Troy Books Publishing
BM Box 8003
London WC1N 3XX

Cover design by Gemma Gary
Cover art by Paul Atlas-Saunders

Printed and bound in Great Britain

For my wonderful wife Tracey, with love, without whose support and encouragement this book would not have grown to be what it has become

ACKNOWLEDGMENTS

My initial work and research into the field of Black Dog folklore was facilitated through access to the archives of the late Theo Brown at the University of Exeter by the then Special Collections Librarian, Madeleine Midgeley. I am in her debt for granting me such prolonged access, which enabled Theo's wonderful collection to be properly brought to light. I am also thankful to the late Dr Hilda Davidson for granting permission for this work to be used and published in this way.

Other researchers have made significant contributions to this project in various ways and I especially thank Janet Bord for donating her archive of Black Dog research to my own and granting permission for its use, to Mike Burgess (owner of the Shuckland website) for sending me his database of sightings for his region and to Dr Simon Sherwood for contributing some of his collection which has been used for background research.

My publishers at Troy Books, Jane Cox and Gemma Gary, have been hugely supportive of the writing process to bring this manuscript to publication and I shall be ever grateful for the lack of a firm deadline in finishing writing!

Whilst not contributing directly to the archive, I would mention the support given to me in general discussion, chat, banter and socialising from some of my close friends in folklore circles – in no particular order Dr Caroline Oates at the Folklore Society, Dr Fiona-Jane Brown, Dr Paul Cowdell, David Waldron and Marc Armitage.

Devon based author Laura Quigley has contributed ideas and discussion on some local aspects of Devon accounts for which I am grateful. To all of my other family, friends and acquaintances who have put up with my general ramblings on the subject over the last few years, thank you. To anyone missed specifically by name, I am grateful for all of the support you have given me.

Finally, I thank my wife Tracey and daughter Alyssa Rose for putting up with the constant movement of paperwork around the house and evenings typing and retyping. Tracey's constant support (she would call it "nagging") and encouragement have turned this project around from being a short study to an extensive work, more fitting of what the subject deserves and she has all of my love for this and everything else.

Contents

Photoplates

between pages 120 -121

Haye Lane, Uplyme, East Devon.
Hoe Benham, Berkshire.
Bar sign depicting the Le Tchan du Bouôlé.
The tomb of Richard Cabel at Buckfastleigh Old Church.
The ruins of Whitby Abbey.
The Black Dog Inn in Black Dog Village, Devon.
The Church at Bungay.
Bungay town weathervane.
The ruins of Dunwich Abbey.
The door of Blythburgh Church with 'claw marks'.
A childhood experience of Dr Simon Sherwood.
The old Black Dog 'obby 'oss.
An image from the Richel collection relating to mandrake pulling.

INTRODUCTION

I fell over the 'Black Dog' by accident. In the 1990s I was introduced to the archives of the late Devon folklorist Theo Brown, which are housed in the University of Exeter Heritage Collections department. My original intention on accessing the archive was to look through her fieldwork on local ghost stories for anything of interest but I became diverted by a large blue ammunition box in which she kept her catalogues of sightings and notes on Black Dog ghosts. On examining the archive in more detail, it became apparent just how much work there was and how little was really known about. In 1958, Theo had written a seminal article for the journal Folklore on Black Dog ghosts but the three draft copies of a book manuscript and catalogue of over two hundred and fifty eyewitness accounts had, in the main, been unused. This seemed a great shame.

It was. Further investigation put me in touch with Dr Hilda Davidson, another eminent folklorist now sadly deceased, with whom I spoke and corresponded. She told me that many people were constantly badgering Theo to finish her book and there was a great sense of disappointment when sadly, due to suffering a stroke, she was unable to continue with her writing. Dr Davidson, responsible for Theo's literary affairs, was keen that the contents should see the light of day and be published. Hence, she granted me permission to do so in whatever way was best, providing they retained an academic standing.

That was the starting point for this book, which I hope will do this initial remit, justice. Written in the time that it was, that initial research has, for reasons of language and similar, needed extensive updating and editing, to be able to integrate it into this wider study. Since the mid to late twentieth century, there have been many changes in the way that we all communicate and the coming together of our once disparate countries through the 'globalisation' of the nations means that there are so many more avenues to explore, eyewitness accounts to examine and comparisons to draw. My own research and collections, therefore, now expand significantly upon these initial works.

Theo Brown lived and worked from the Exeter area of Devon, in the United Kingdom, for most of her life. She was the daughter of a Welsh scholar who was later made a department head of the British Museum. As an infant, Theo was placed in an orphanage where she stayed for two years before being adopted by the Langford Brown family who lived at Barton Hall in Kingskerswell, Devon – a large country residence built by H. Langford Brown, Theo's adoptive father. It was here that she was educated, in the main, by governesses. It was here also, that her interest in the subject was most likely sparked whilst sitting at the dinner table listening to her father recount his tales, since one concerned a ghostly black dog which he had seen (and which we will examine in the first chapter).

The study of psychic phenomena has been growing and developing since the nineteenth century when the popularity of the Victorian séance began to catch the attention of the scientific community. Since that time it has branched into many diverse areas: UFOs, telepathy, psychokinesis, cryptozoology – just a few examples of the many fields of study. Of all the subjects spanning the "paranormal banner", ghosts probably come out as the most popular and timeless.

After years of continued study by scientists and academics, psychologists, parapsychologists and amateur investigators employing rigorous techniques with meticulous care and integrity, the conclusions are roughly what one might expect: ghosts may or may not exist. Science cannot always provide us with an answer. It may be that it never will. Even if it does, many people will choose to ignore it and hold onto their own beliefs. This in itself is by no means unimportant, but it does position psychic research in something of a cul-de-sac where new approaches need to be developed and tried. The field of folklore as an area of study has a lot to offer. In this approach the question "Do ghosts exist?" is not posed. If they do exist, they are not the concern of the folklorist. Folklore is primarily concerned with the basic beliefs and rituals of human beings as emanations of the human mind rather than whether or not they coincide with actual external entities.

The study of folklore is very often the examination of symbolism and symbolic interpretation changes over time. Religious views are less widely held in some countries now than they were in the past and hence fewer people are likely to draw on religious themes in their interpretation of events that they class as out of the ordinary. It may be the case that some interpretation comes from a shared or collective subconscious, as tradition is born out of such things but a key indicator to interpretation is that the observer needs some form of comparator. It is these comparators that are likely to change over time.

Consider fairies. In Victorian times and earlier, people spoke of being 'pixie-led', or being 'away with the fairies'. They would report absences for long periods of time, whereas they had been away for only a short time or vice versa. Fairies were said to take human babies and substitute changelings in their place. In recent times, people speak of alien abduction, of human/alien hybridisation and again, of lost times periods which are not quite what they seem. There are many parallels.

Both fairies and grey aliens, the most common type reported, can have large almond-shaped eyes, pale skin, large heads and delicate bodies. People abducted by fairies report an earthy smell; people abducted by aliens have often reported a smell similar to cinnamon. There are parallels between glowing lights in the fairy world and alien craft.

Culture can play an important part in the interpretation of alleged paranormal phenomena. In these cases, an unknown "something" has happened to the abductees and their interpretation of what has happened, or that of the people around them, has been drawn from the culture of the day. Modern science-fiction stories and culture have translated the older stories, such that the abductors move from being fairies to extra-terrestrial beings. In their role as a 'decoder' of such reports, the folklorist can be seen to have a valuable part to play in furthering psychic research.

Many ghosts appear or behave in a way that seems less human than symbolic – without a head, or floating in the air, for example. No-one could suppose these to be representational photographs. Symbolism is a language and so we need to ask who is trying to say what, and to whom? Only then shall we be in a position to ask the question to which the enquiry is leading: If ghosts do exist, why?

Symbolism is a subject that is of great importance in studies of, particularly, religion and psychology. One of the greatest difficulties raised by the scientific revolution is that we have to some extent abandoned the ancient system of traditional symbolism; we no longer have a "common culture" in an unspoken language that all through our history men and women have taken for granted. This is partly because we do not live so closely to nature as we used to and, therefore, not so closely to each other.

Images appear spontaneously in dreams and fantasy and their interpretation can be seen as important to our inner health. We have to remember that an unknown, though proportionately large, quantity of the mind lies in the unconscious part of it. Between that and the conscious mind is a threshold, and the only communication between the two is by means of symbolic language.

It is possible that, if spirits existed, they could make contact with the human observer at the unconscious level and only be able to force their way across the threshold of consciousness in a disguised and symbolic form. Such 'beings' would have no form of their own and their choice of image would therefore be limited to the selection in the mind of the person experiencing the phenomenon. These factors may explain the apparent subjectivity of many experiences. However, there may well be an external cause. Further, if the entity is purposive then the image selected must be that which is most suitable to express it. If we can propose this rule then the kind of symbol is of the utmost importance for deducing the character, intention and identity of the transmitting agent, whether it be human or "other-worldly". This is, of course, only a speculative theory.

Many symbols that come up in dreams and the like, have a purely personal interpretation but it appears that, although we have consciously forsaken the language of symbolism and do not understand our own imaginings, our subconscious still speaks to us in images. As individuals we are obliged to relearn this primitive symbolism to understand.

There are many reports of ghost animals. Whereas some of these may be ghosts of real animals, others may never have lived and could be images of something formless in the way previously described. Such entities are perceived as different creatures by various people, as we should expect if the image is not seen objectively through the physical eyes but enters via the subconscious and emerges to consciousness.

This book is concerned with the 'Black Dog' ghost. Many symbols such as the horse and dove are common. Because people are familiar with them, they think they know the answers before the questions have been asked and so are blinded to an objective view. The Black Dog is a far more unexpected image. It actually occurs very frequently as a ghost or in dreams, but in some isolation. Few people have ever thought about it, other than perhaps in reading The Hound of the Baskervilles.

This is an ideal starting point. Instead of beginning with a theory and planning to conform to it, we can begin, almost blindfold, with the material. Through analysis we can extract the internal evidence: What do the Black Dogs tell us about themselves?

It is telling that Black Dogs have been sighted, felt, heard and experienced in an unnatural way by people for near on a millennia now and yet people stumble across information about them by chance, when attempting to provide themselves with an explanation for what has occurred. Phrases are often along the lines of this one, recorded in April 2014:

> *"I ran across your request for Black Dog sightings ... and since the topic has been on my mind ever since learning recently that my experiences aren't unique, I thought I would record mine for you."*
> (Laura Christensen, personal correspondence, 23 April 2014)

Finding out that they are not alone in their experiences is often surprising to the people concerned. They are relieved that others have had shared, or similar experiences and telling their story brings a sense of closure. This was true in Laura's case, which is examined in more detail in the chapter 'Protective Dogs'. She ended by saying that she had wanted to share her experience for some time, but didn't know how to – despite there being nearly one thousand years of experiences to draw on!

This is in large part due to the fact that there have been very few serious studies on the phenomenon in this time. There are only a small number of researchers today working in any depth on the phenomena and these are adding to the work of another small number of past studies. In the early to middle part of the twentieth century, most of the collection and interpretation of data was undertaken by three folklorists: Ethel Rudkin, Ruth L. Tongue and Theo Brown.

The phenomena of the Black Dog ghost is not a British one, or indeed attached to any particular country, religion or any other social group. It is, however, in the United Kingdom that the widest diversity of the types of Black Dog ghost can be found and, therefore, they provide the broadest possible set of case studies, which can hope to inform anyone experiencing them, or with an interest, wherever in the world they may come across the motif. It is here we can find Black Dogs that may be good, evil or portentous, attached to a road, a house or a family, protective, mythological, normal looking or really rather strange.

No book can be large enough to describe the constellation of history, tradition, topography, religion, social conditions or personal psychology that make up the milieu of one psychic experience. Writers have shown the difficulty of understanding psychic phenomena without a very complete knowledge of the psychology of the person involved and the group in which they live. Unfortunately, however, in the majority of cases, the bare story is all that there is to go on. Material such as that included here, therefore, has to be accepted at face value with this warning borne fully in mind but this should not cause us a problem. We are not undertaking a scientific analysis of testimony. We are rather interested in trying to decode and understand the symbolism, thoughts and feelings of those involved.

We will start at the beginning, with a general overview of the phenomena of the spectral Black Dog.

A General Description of
DOG GHOSTS

The dog is unique in folklore terms. All domesticated animals functioned as an extension of man and many still do to a lesser extent. In ancient times they supplied hides for warmth or protection, they gave food for strength and to prolong life. Bones were used as weapons or tools and horns provided a more varied voice before the natural one was developed. In later development, cats killed the vermin which evaded human capture and horses lent speed and strength for journeys, or in times of war. But the dog is somewhat different.

The dog was certainly domesticated as far back as Mesolithic times and there is evidence which suggests that, in fact, they were kept as pets even in the Upper Palaeolithic. This means that Kipling's proposal of the dog as "Man's First Friend" may be literally true and that of all the creature companions, it is the canine that has associated itself with mankind from the earliest possible times. He may certainly be considered 'Man's Best Friend', emerging from the primeval forest as a fellow huntsman. The dog contributed speed and cunning to the chase, his bite to the battle and his bark to the lonely fireside.

Dog ghosts appear to have been seen all over the world. The interpretation of them, of course, depends on the religious views of each community. Certain races, such as the Jewish, Arab and the Protestant movement in Europe, hold the dog to be unclean. Others - the Celtic, the Roman and the Africans - regard ghostly dogs as part of the family. Phantom dogs are common in Europe and hence wherever there are European settlers, in other continents. The West African slaves took their ghostly dogs to America and, in Texas at least, these dogs are never black but usually appear white, or sometimes yellow.

In Protestant Germany and Scandinavia the ghost dog is nearly always diabolic. In the former case, for example, the devil is said to appear in the form of a black dog. This is also the case in Catholic Eire, although in most Catholic countries it is hardly regarded at all by the Church. In Britain, which as discussed in the Introduction will comprise a significant part of this book due to its wide range of examples, there are two types of creature. Firstly, there is the Black Dog, which is usually just like any ordinary large dog to look at and secondly, there is the 'Barguest' type. The Barguest appears in various shapes, but generally that of a dog. It is dangerous and ominous to meet it, especially head on. Sometimes it lacks a head; sometimes it has only one eye in the middle of its forehead. The Barguest occurs in wide areas of East Anglia and in the North of England, from Cumberland down to the Yorkshire Dales - as far south as the Peak District.

There are some overlaps between the traits of these two types of ghostly dog but, for the most part, we can consider them as separate genera (to borrow a scientific term from their living counterparts). We will examine both in great detail later in this book, so a summary alone is useful for now.

The ordinary looking Black Dog occurs sporadically all over Britain and we can be thankful that a small number of folklorists from the early and middle parts of the twentieth century collected a wealth of reports. Theo Brown attempted a distribution map as part of her seminal article on the subject for the journal Folklore in 1958 but this is of limited use. The map showed thicker concentrations where researchers had collected sightings: Mrs E.H. Rudkin in Lincolnshire; Miss Ruth L. Tongue for West Somerset and herself in Devon. The Rev. W.P. Witcutt collected many accounts for Staffordshire and Warwickshire where the dog is often called the 'Padfoot'. As there are pockets of Gaelic elements in this area he surmised that the word might derive from badda fuath, the Gaelic for 'fairy dog' but it is more likely an onomatopoeic word to describe its character in the same way as the Lancashire 'Trash' or 'Gytrash' is believed to be adopted from the curious sound made by the hound's footfall.

In more recent times, collections of sightings and analysis have been undertaken by another small group of researchers in the main, notably Janet Bord, Ivan Bunn, Michael Burgess (who manages the excellent Shuckland website for East Anglian examples), Bob Trubshaw (who compiled the useful collection of articles comprising the book Explore Phantom Black Dogs), Dr Simon Sherwood and myself. There are, of course, others who have written on the subject but space does not permit name-checking them all. Suffice to say their work is easy to track down and extremely valuable.

The breed of dog sighted varies from the vast 'Newfoundland' to quite small terriers or spaniels but they are usually reminiscent of retrievers or mastiffs. In these cases they are commonly described as larger than any normal dog. "As big as a calf" or "as big as a donkey" are typical similes. Just a few are not seen but heard, felt or smelt.

Although it is usually alone when it is sighted, there are several reports of ghost dogs accompanying their deceased masters. Whereas the Barguest type of dog (or Shuck as it is called in East Anglia) is invariably horrific in some way, the Black Dog is either neutral or friendly and protective. This is the case, for example, in Lincolnshire which seems strange when it adjoins the East Anglian Shuck area.

It is important to bear in mind these differences in character to fully understand the subject, particularly given the propensity for less knowledgeable writers to always use the Barguest type of animal when referring to the tradition. Journalists, in particular, will always tend to move to the "hound of hell" description if they need to reference Black Dog legends – it is far more exciting than a friendly animal. We shall see an excellent example of this at the end of this book.

The popular superstitious conception of the Black Dog is that it is an omen of death but collating the reports and traditions actually shows that at least half the dogs are harmless. They are frequently protectors of lonely women and timid men walking along sinister roads (or, in older reports, when passing footpads and robbers). There are two distinct areas that these protective dogs seem to favour - the North part of Lincolnshire and Tyneside – although, this is not to say that people experiencing a meeting with a Black Dog in other areas, do not report these traits.

There are six main categories that are frequently reported upon in sightings and stories of ghost dogs. Some of these refer to the Black Dog, some to the Barguest and some apply to both types of apparition.

1. Size: There is often something unusual about the size of the animal. As previously mentioned it is often uncommonly large. An eyewitness account recorded in

private correspondence dated 7th February 1960 demonstrates this type of description:

> *"About fifty odd years ago, I was returning home late one evening from a tea-party at a farm with my little girl on a donkey (well known as Romeo). We were taking a short cut to the furze brake just across the river, where the donkey was always unsaddled and turned loose. As we were going down the lane by Okehampton Castle, a huge black dog as big as a pony, jumped out of the Castle grounds and stood glaring at us. And though Romeo was always anxious to get back to his grazing ground, nothing would induce him to go on, even after the dog had disappeared. We had to make a very long detour to reach home."*

(Mrs. Grace Pearse in personal correspondence to Theo Brown, 7th February 1960)

More unusually, at Uplyme in Devon the dog swells in size until it is as high as a house or tree, gradually thinning out until it disperses (see Chapter 2).

2. Colour: The usual tone is black, although there are some variations in reports where dogs have been white, yellow and in one case, red. It may seem a misnomer to be discussing apparitions of Black Dogs and yet to include these other reports. It would be more accurate to use the term 'ghost dogs' for the field of study as these other cases are included because there is no real difference in details apart from the colour of the coat. Virtually all dog apparition reports are black and so over the hundreds of years that the phenomena has been observed the term Black Dog has naturally been adopted.

3. Physical details: The coat observed on the apparition may be gleaming and smooth or it may be remarkably rough and shaggy. When it is felt only and not seen, the hair may feel bristly - more like a pig's than a hound's. The tail is usually long and thin. The eyes, if they appear to be abnormal, are huge. A recurring key phrase in many reports from the early and mid parts of the twentieth century describes them as "like

tea saucers" or "as big as dinner plates" shining brilliantly, or glowing red. It is of significant interest that these phrases come up again and again, both in traditional reports and in eyewitness accounts, as it shows how the symbolism travels and passes from person to person, without anyone realising that it is happening.

In point of fact, we find the expression in what is probably the earliest recording of a sighting in Britain. This comes from the Anglo Saxon Chronicle, the earliest known history of England written in the native tongue. The document was probably first compiled for King Alfred before being sent to monasteries across Britain for copying around 892AD. Its first version spanned the period from the birth of Christ to Alfred's reign and comprised an official history of the country but the individual copies were then kept updated in each location and began to take on more independent histories. Most versions end around the Norman Conquest of 1066 but one continues until 1154 and it is in this version that we find the mention of the dog. Many writers quote a common translation of this passage, which reads that:

> *"Many men both saw and heard a great number of huntsmen hunting. The huntsmen were black, huge and hideous and rode on black horses and on black he-goats and their hounds were jet black with eyes like saucers and horrible".*

Even in this very early account, we find reference to the size of the eyes. We also, however, must note an interesting etymological problem here, as the word 'saucer' derives from the 14th century and hence cannot be a direct translation from the original document. The correct translation, in fact, reads that the hounds were "black and big-eyed and loathsome". The meaning carries though, with the later recurring description having been juxtaposed onto the original translation, highlighting again its significance. Unfortunately, most writers still tend to quote the mistranslated version.

We find the size of the eyes also being commented on in other places, such as the children's tale The Magic Tinderbox. Even now, in a number of more recent reports from the early part of the twenty first century, the size of the eyes is still commented on but often a yellow hue is described.

4. Head: If the ghost is not realistic then there may be something odd about the head. In one case at least, at Kildonan in Scotland, treasure hidden in a pool is said to be guarded by a dog with two heads. The stagnant pool, measuring ten yards by three, was said to contain a pot of gold. Legend says that a tenant once drained the pool in search of the gold but every midnight thereafter, the dog would howl and the noise did not stop until the farmer, whose land it was on, filled it in again.

This tale immediately draws to mind a parallel with Cerberus, the multi-headed hell hound which was a guardian of the underworld in Greek Mythology. There are a number of reports where Black Dogs are said to be guardians of treasure, and this is especially the case in Scotland.

At Knaith in Lincolnshire, a murdered woman known as 'Mrs Dog' appears from a hill as a Black Dog with a woman's face. The story goes that Mrs Dog was a rich elderly widow who lived alone in an isolated cottage by the road. One day a traveller broke into the cottage and killed the woman (presumably because he had heard of her wealth although this is not made clear).

In Cornwall, it is sometimes said that Black Dogs are the ghosts of wicked men and all have the human features reproduced. As a concession to the truly horrible sight that this would be, these heads are usually invisible and this is said to explain the quantities of headless dogs reported! These are also traditional in the Lake District and in Norfolk. There are also a few sightings of dogs with a pair of horns.

5. Oddities: Some ghost dogs appear to have a chain attached to their collars, although the other end never seems to be secured. One or two are reported as standing or walking on their hind legs. One report in the Transactions of

the Devonshire Association tell that at Newton St. Cyres in Devon, a girl was murdered by her uncle in a cottage, leaving an indelible bloodstain. A resident who lived at the cottage told that if the outside door was open, a Black Dog would sometimes walk past on its hind legs at a particular time. A further piece from the same publication fifty years later, reports that at Ilsington, a Black Dog haunts the road to Lenda Farm. The Dog is said to have appeared to the uncle of a local farmer who said that it walked along beside the hedge, remaining on its hind legs and that it seemed *"about the size of a calf"*. He was apparently driving a pony and trap at the time of the incident and the pony showed every sign of terror. In cases of this type, the origin of the story could often be traced back to someone said to be guising the part, as in witchcraft.

Speaking dogs are known. Dobb Park Lodge in Lancashire was originally one out of a collection of three hunting lodges. The building, which was scheduled as a Grade II listed ancient monument in 1997, was said to have been the property of the Duchy of Lancaster, situated in the valley of the Washburn on the southern slope. We will examine a legend concerning a speaking dog here later Chapter Nine.

Another speaking dog, from Lincolnshire, was known as the Belle Hole Boggart (a Boggart being a mischievous shape-shifting spirit common in some of the northern areas of England). The district nurse had been visiting Belle Hole, a farm about a mile west of Kirton, where she had been tending the children. As she had been giving them their supper, the children had been speaking of the Boggart and asked the nurse if she was not scared of meeting the creature on her walk back to Kirton. The nurse's response to questions about what she would do if she did, was that she *"shall put 'im i'my pocket"*. On her way home later, the Dog was said to have appeared and run around the district nurse saying, *"put me in yer pocket, put me in yer pocket"*. One theory suggests that the nurse was hearing a train passing on the line nearby, the noise of the wheels on the gaps in the rails being carried on the wind blowing from the north or northwest and making a sound with a similar rhythm.

6. Function: This may amount to almost anything, from standing still to accompanying a pedestrian or pacing a vehicle along a road. It may arrive suddenly from nowhere, it may leap over a wall, you may meet it, be overtaken from behind by it, or it may just cross in front of you. When it leaves, it may vanish or sink slowly into the ground, generally by some landmark such as a tree, gap in the hedge or into a solid object.

Although these six aspects are often mentioned, as we have just noted with the descriptions of the eyes, they have tended to vary over time. It is interesting to note that in the reports gathered by the folklorists of the twentieth century, the language used is very accepting of the phenomena witnessed or felt. The witnesses seem generally quite informed about the nature, legend or folklore of the Black Dog and in their correspondence they tend to start quite matter-of-factly: "I saw the Black Dog a few weeks ago. I was out riding on my horse..." On the other hand, more recent reports often start, as with Laura Christensen's example in the Introduction, with the witness stating that they had got in touch because they had been searching the internet for information on ghostly dogs, or that they were unaware that other people had seen them.

This seems to suggest that the Black Dog is no longer as well known as it was as a folkloric image. Remembering what we have already noted about the language of symbolism having been lost in these modern times, is there still a folk memory surviving in the collective consciousness, or is something else at work?

Methods of comparison are important when we look at these shifting descriptions, as we saw with the examination of fairy reports against alien abductions. Size has already been discussed above as an attribute worthy of investigation and by this we mean that the Black Dog often appears to be larger than a domestic animal. In accounts from eyewitnesses in the early to mid part of the twentieth century, for example, people often used phrases such as "as big as a calf" or "as big as a 'Newfoundland'" when describing the size of the dog. The recurring descriptions are essentially embedded in the commonplace of the time. Many more people lived on and worked the land and so the calf as a comparator is quite natural.

Many of the more recent reports are tending to use a different comparator and have phrases such as "big as a wolf" or that the dog resembles a wolf in some way. Historically, aside from the saucer-ness, the eyes are often described as glowing or fiery and where they are abnormal, they are red. More recent accounts have jet black or yellow eyes added to these descriptions and many describe them as having evil intent.

Another interesting change goes along with these more modern reports. There are descriptions of growling, snarling and scratching claws. These auditory phenomena are of great interest as it is very rare in all of the collected historical accounts for sound to accompany Black Dog sightings. In the odd occasions where it does, it is usually the padding of the feet that is described. There is only the very sporadic bark or growl.

What might be happening here? We can perhaps argue that modern entertainment is playing a part. Historically, television and film dealt with tamer subjects and from the 'penny dreadfuls' through to the mid part of the twentieth century, horror stories in literature tended to deal with different themes to the modern day. Horror films and books have become much more prevalent and much less 'tame' and themes such as lycanthropy, demonism and the like are not only dealt with more often but are far more blatant. In his book, Tracing the Chupacabra, Benjamin Radford suggests that reports are much influenced by modern movies and the same may be true here. Modern consumers of entertainment have much more of a stomach for horror themes and may draw on these entertainments more, in the decoding of the symbolism surrounding Black Dog folklore.

By far the most numerous quantity of Black Dog apparitions are on roads or pathways. Various reasons can be suggested for this. They are usually sighted at night, when humans would naturally be following a road and therefore would see only what occurred in their path. A dog wandering home from a day's business would be just as likely to use the road.

Some specimens are traditionally believed to patrol certain stretches of road. The Cornish 'carrier' is believed to be the ghost of a dog that always accompanied a carrier on his life-long journeys between Liskeard and Launceston. The carrier is compelled to travel as many Saturdays after death as before and it has been suggested that the dog acts as his protector. Seen near Berriow Bridge in North Hill, Middlewood, miners tied a rope across the road to check the dog but at midnight there was such a commotion that people had to get up and cut the rope. Many of the reports of patrolling dogs may be the guardians of such carriers. A similar example of a guardian is found at Roborough in Devon and was described by folklore collector Sarah Hewett in her 1900 book Nummits & Crummits:

> "A man was walking from Princetown to Plymouth on a December evening. On the Plymouth side of the reservoir he heard and saw a black dog, the size of a Newfoundland. He tried to pat it but his hand passed straight through. Frightened, he hurried on, with the dog staying with him until he reached the crossroads. There was a loud report at this point, and a blinding flash and the man fell senseless to the ground. There is a tradition of murder at this point, and the victim's dog tries to kill every passerby in the hope of catching the murderer. The dog is described as having "great glassy eyes" and sulphurous breath."

There are also many cases reported of huge black dogs that run alongside horses and carriages and suddenly disappear when they come to the end of their patrol. These road dogs are significant enough to have their own chapter later in the book.

The difficulty in collecting folklore such as the stories examined in this book is that the people who have the information do not necessarily recognise their own time-worn memories and direct questioning may not be of much use in producing the story - a more oblique approach may sometimes need to be adopted. This, however, produces eyewitness accounts which then run the risk of being criticised by any respectable psychic researcher because they were not recorded within a day or so of the event or because they are not accompanied by supporting statements from independent witnesses.

However, the purpose of this book is not to approach the topic from the point of view of a psychic researcher but from a folkloric angle. Therefore, it is quite acceptable in this case to accept the accounts at face value because this is how stories and traditions are passed on. In fact, it is still not a problem when taking this approach if the stories have become distorted by the action of the individual's tendency towards myth-making, as this is part of the interest of folklore research.

Before we examine the folklore of Black Dogs in more detail, we will start with a short selection of these eyewitness accounts which will also serve as useful examples of the general descriptions we have already cited. Telling of their experiences can often be a comfort to the person involved, who may have been worried by experiences which they could never relate for fear of derision. These experiences prove so upsetting that the person puts them out of their mind until hearing something which reminds them of it much later.

One example is that of a story recalled by a woman and her husband after hearing a talk on ghost dogs at the time they had been on a motoring holiday. They were crossing Wiltshire late one evening and became lost somewhere between Maud Heath's Causeway and Chippenham. As they were getting tired, they decided that they would look for a hotel but came to a village with an attractive old church, which they instantly wanted to explore.

They entered the church, which was already darkening, by the south door. The font was close by and the vicar of the parish was standing there, so the husband, a well-known physicist with rational views, courteously engaged him in conversation. His wife turned right and proceeded slowly up the aisle towards the east end, which was by then in almost total darkness. Suddenly, ahead of her, she heard a clinking of metal and footsteps, and into her vision strode a knight in full armour with a huge black dog at his heels. He walked rapidly down the aisle and the woman automatically stood aside to let him pass. Too astounded to comment, she merely looked back to see what her husband and the vicar would make of this but as he marched both the knight and his dog faded away. The professor and the vicar steadily went on chatting, neither having seen nor heard anything.

The woman assumed that the whole thing was her imagination, brought on by fatigue and she did not like to make a fool of herself by saying anything. She was considerably upset that the hallucination had been so vivid that she had actually stepped aside to let the man pass. In fact, she purposely did not enquire as to the name of the village in which they had stopped and did her best to forget the whole thing. The story, which originally happened in the 1930s, was recorded in personal correspondence years later with the proviso that it was told on the strict condition that names were withheld. Although the name of the woman involved has since been published in the public domain, I believe it is respectful to honour the original wishes which brought the story to light in the first place and hence it remains withheld here.

As already mentioned in the Introduction to this book, folklorist Theo Brown's interest in the Black Dog was piqued by a story told by her adoptive father, an Oxford graduate described as factual, down-to-earth and not given to imagining things. He recorded the story, for which no date is given but is likely to have been before his marriage in 1907, in his papers:

> *"There is a lane that leads from the village of Coffinswell to Kingskerswell33 Cross, and this is called Willowpark Lane … It crosses a stream, and the Parson who used to live at Coffinswell told me that he had frequently heard people talking just as he came to this stream; he had gone in to the fields at each side of the lane, on these occasions, but he never found anyone there. One Sunday at about 8.30 on an autumn evening, just as it was dusk, I was returning from Coffinswell Church. I was late and walking very fast. Just as I came down the steep hill, on the Coffinswell side of the valley, I saw a man and a dog about seventy yards in front of me. I overtook them, and got up to within about three yards of them. They went round a sharp bend in the lane, and absolutely vanished. The hedges here were both seven of eight feet high, and it was impossible that they could have got over them in anything under thirty or forty seconds, and I was not two seconds behind them. The man was very thick set, and had on breeches and gaiters, with a brown coloured tail coat and a billy-cock hat. The dog which was about the size of a sheep dog baffles all description, as it was a rough-coated mongrel of the worst description. I was so close behind the man's back that I could see the seam in his coat, but the dog was closer to me. I did not feel at all alarmed, although I felt that what I had seen was something supernatural."*

These examples seem to be some kind of timeslip which seems to defy rational explanation where you suddenly glimpse a sector of past time at a particular locality. In neither case was there any emotion involved - both happened at evening in a half light and both those involved were presumably tired after a long day. That is all we know. There seems to be no significance to them for the observers.

The following examples seem to have a little more significance attached to them. An author of books on sea matters wrote this vivid account in a letter dated 1959:

"When I lived at Chideock, Dorset, before World War II, walking home to my cottage late one winter's night from Morecombelake, with a naval friend, we were literally 'dogged' by a large black animal which padded along behind us, all the way. It was an uncanny experience, and I shall never forget it; it was a great deal more uncanny when, as we reached the old graveyard at the crossroads (to North Chideock and Seaton) we stood silent and watched the hound pad its way towards an enormous gravestone and disappear before our eyes. It was a vividly bright moonlight night."

Crosscombe Manor, at Trevellas near St. Agnes on the North Cornwall coast is a Tudor house on the site of an old monastery which was destroyed by Henry VIII. It has smuggling traditions and is reputedly haunted but with no clearly defined ghost. Smells of upturned soil, lilies or roses have been reported on the staircase and in the hall of the building. Around 1943 a new owner, Mrs Garth-Heyworth, bought Crosscombe Manor and used it as a guest house for summer visitors. Mrs Garth-Heyworth was descended from the Garths of Shirebank Hall in Lancashire and had a family banshee in the form of a black dog. She had a (living) dog called Psyche, half-staghound and half-greyhound, with rough black hair. In personal correspondence dated 1960 she told of seeing a ghost dog at the manor:

"A few years ago I was busy getting some new curtains machined, and my woman had cleaned down upstairs already for the people coming in that day, and shut all the room doors to keep my old dog from running into the rooms and jumping on the beds - a habit of hers. It was a hot day, and I had the doors to the hall open, and I was busy sewing when I glanced up to see a big black hound (like a staghound) rush through the door and upstairs. I jumped up, called to my husband (who was in another room) - 'Who's let Psyche loose?' and thinking it was my hound Psyche, ran upstairs to catch her, thinking of her dirty paws on my clean beds. Well, I saw her turn the first six stairs, but when

I got there, and to the top of the flight, there was nothing there, and I went into every room - of which every door was tight shut - but there was no sign of a dog anywhere. I got quite a strange feeling when there was no dog to be found, and rushed down to my husband who was then asking what I was making such a fuss about, as our dog was asleep in her kennel in a shed the other side of the house. I wouldn't believe him and went round to look for myself - she was chained up for the afternoon, as we always did when visitors were expected ...

"Then one moonlight night I saw the same sort of dog running round our lily pond in the garden and I watched from my bedroom window and saw it take a twelve-foot jump over a high bush hedge and vanish in the jump."

If the black dog was the family fetch, it is odd that no death or calamity followed. The door past which the ghost ran seems to have had something unpleasant about it. One visitor, quite new to the place, felt a terrible choking sensation as she passed under the lintel.

The dogs in these examples vanished in circumstances that suggest that they were beings in their own right and were acting with some kind of purpose which was in all probability independent of the person who observed them.

One common theme running through these accounts is the fact that none of the localities had a tradition of a local Black Dog haunt. Through the rest of this book we will examine more closely the traditions of dog ghosts and more particularly, those of the Black Dog folklore.

DOGS OF THE WESTCOUNTRY

The phantom hounds that haunt the west of England are a very useful collection with which to begin our examination of the subject, as they are representative of nearly every type of apparition which we will be looking at in more detail over the coming chapters.

In West Somerset, on the Quantocks, on Exmoor and on the Blackdown Hills the dogs appear near prehistoric burials and other various types of ancient site. One Black Dog is said to haunt a lane on Blackdown where there was a Roman lookout post, and Blackdown Barrows are also reputed to be haunted by Black Dogs, although there are no reports which give direct confirmation of this legend.

Some apparitions are reported as having been seen by hunting people in these areas. On Exmoor in North Devon one is said to be sighted by hunters if they ride too near to the cairns. The folklorist Ruth L. Tongue collected another report in 1957 from the Quantocks, which she described in a letter to Theo Brown:

"A rider returning in late autumn dusk over the Quantock Hills after stag-hunting found his weary horse in a sweat of fear

*and saw a large black dog pacing alongside about ten feet away.
The horse was too terrified to swerve and gallop but had to be
urged to walk on over a distance of about a mile. The rider said
he was sweating in cold terror too. The dog seemed to come from
one cairn and follow along to disappear to another one. At once
the horse broke into a gallop and arrived home exhausted. As
my hunting friend does not want to be laughed at I cannot give
the locality, but judging by the impression made on him and the
nerve of his horse, they certainly both saw the Black Dog this
year (1957)."*

The Quantock Black Dog, or maybe Dogs as we cannot
tell if there is one roaming or a collection of them in the area,
has generated many reports over the years. The following is
a small selection of these from the archives:

*"My father could never get a hunter up the Combe, nor could
anyone else. They always went another way round, and hounds
would never set on there. I hate the Combe. It always gives me
a queer feeling; I won't go near it. My Father hunted all his
life and was a hard unimaginative man but he would never ride
that way."*
(President, Cossington Women's Institute, 1961)

*"I was in the middle of a talk on Ghost lore and had
asked anyone to question me when just after a reference to
Black Dogs I was interrupted by an eager member: 'How
large is the Black Dog and what does it look like?' I gave
her the traditional calf size, rough coated, saucer-eyed beast
and she at once replied in relief from her perplexity: 'We
didn't see its eyes but it must have been the Black Dog we saw
last Thursday (30th May, 1963). We were walking up from
the Castle of Comfort to the top (past the site of Walford's
Gibbet) and it crossed in front of us just where the woods
end. It came out of the trees and into the woods. It was like
an enormous black Alsatian - yes, as big as a calf. We were
puzzled by it. It was so queer.'"*

(Ruth L. Tongue in personal correspondence to Theo Brown, 12th June 1963)

"The Black Dog who guards the ancient trackway from West Quantoxhead towards Crowcombe was sighted rushing down the steep sides of the Deer Park one late autumn evening. It was seen by a motor-cyclist who could not make out what animal it was: 'about the size of a large pig - and what puzzled me was its coat looked like ruffled feathers. It was black and something like a dog, it moved like one but I have never met anything like it before or since.' This was an unusual extension of the Dog's known patrol."

"The Quantock Black Dog can be friendly and has been known to guard and accompany straying small village children picking 'worts' or mushrooms. I have heard of cottage women whose toddlers wandered about the nearby coombe, who never worried because 'the girt old black dog up-over took care of they'. They did not refer to a farm dog."

(Both from Ruth L. Tongue in personal correspondence to Theo Brown, 19th September 1960)

And finally, recorded in the original dialect from a farmer's wife at Buncombe Farm:

"Oh yes, I've rode a pony over the hills all times of the day or night, and there's one combe they just won't go. You can't ride'n nor lead'en - they just won't, nor our sheep dogs wouldn't neither. The broom squire is still alive near Over Stowey. Did'ee know en? Knowledgeable with beasts and herbs they was, specially the old man. He died recently."

In Street, Somerset, there is a report of one of the rarer apparitions of a differently coloured dog - in this case white. It was said to have been seen by two brothers at Street House, which (probably apocryphally) is supposed to have a tunnel running from it to Glastonbury. The men saw the dog sitting opposite a stove, from which position it rose and left through the door. Three weeks later their father died, although a second appearance of the animal did not lead to a death.

In Dorset the dogs are much scarcer, although there is a further report of a white dog in this county. In personal correspondence with Theo Brown, dated 23rd May 1960, T.C. Lethbridge records:

> *"The incident happened at Manston in Dorset. She (the witness) was staying at a house which was either in the churchyard or close beside it when she went for one of her usual toddles in the evening. Suddenly a smallish white and yellow dog ran close past her and disappeared..."*

When looking briefly at the function of some dog apparitions in Chapter 1 we considered those 'road dogs' that are considered to patrol stretches of the highway for some reason, and these appear to be more common in Cornwall. Miss Barbara C. Spooner collected these reports, such as the Liskeard carrier cited previously, and the following example from Callington where the dog starts at Mark Valley Mine:

> *"A man was supposedly killed in the mine and his name was remembered until recently. The dog ghost is described as big as a yearling, with eyes as tea-cups ... flaming. The route is from Mark Valley Mine 'through Rillamill, up Sellars and past Two Gates in Linkinhorne, to Stoke Climsland. And at Two Gates he was seen by a woman and man driving home in the dark, a hundred or more years ago.' As they approached, it leapt over a 'way-soil' heap and vanished from sight."*

Another dog that seems to follow a road system occurs in North Devon, where the Black Dog of Torrington has been plotted along a line which follows either old roads or ancient tracks from Copplestone, near Crediton, running north-west to Torrington. We will examine this case in detail in Chapter

6 which is devoted to Road Dogs as it is probably the best plotted of all the 'travelling' apparitions. Similarly there is a local legend of the ghost at Chittlehampton that maintains that it ran from there westwards, also to Great Torrington.

The Chittlehampton terminus is associated with Denys Rolle, an 18th century eccentric squire, who had houses there and also in Torrington. He frequently walked between the two. In 1797, whilst on one of these walks, he dropped dead and the Black Dog was said to have appeared and continued the walk. It is evident that the later historical fact was attached to the earlier legend, apparently as a partial rationalisation to explain such a pointless haunting. Taking as an assumption the fact that this may often happen, then we must look at all later 'historical' etiological legends in this light. Where a ghost is conveniently connected with a story we should look around for an alternative and much more ancient cause. We may not find one as ghosts are born every day, in recent times as in prehistory. But we should always be on our guard against obvious and too-easy explanations.

For instance, there is a piece of woodland called Collingbourne Woods to the east of Collingbourne Ducis in Wiltshire which has a Black Dog ghost associated with it. A possibly recent story tells that a murderer on the run from the police tried hiding in the woods and that "he had dark hair when he went in, and when he came out he was white". When the police apprehended him he told them that he had seen a black dog in the woods and that it had blazing eyes. In older records of folklore of the area there is a dog which is attached to White Lane which is in the same area. We can make a relatively safe assumption that the story of the criminal may have been mapped onto, or draws from, the previous accounts in a similar way to the story of Denys Rolle being attached to an earlier legend.

There is a further interesting complication in this Wiltshire example though. John Wilcock, writing in his book A Guide to Occult Britain states that the A346/A338 road running south from Marlborough around Collingbourne Kingston is haunted by a Black Dog with bright saucer-like eyes. In the eighteenth century this dog was said to have appeared to two murderers who were trying to evade capture by the police. It scared them such that they ran further up the road where they were caught. The story of the murderer in Collingbourne Woods may therefore draw from multiple stories as there is an obvious connection also with this historic story of the two criminals.

Many things happen on the site of a haunting. Some may reinforce the haunt, but in view of the irrational quality of haunting it is far more likely that a recent event may blot out a primitive or intuitive origin.

Such a case is the ghost of Lady Howard of Fitzford, Tavistock. She was the daughter of Sir John Fitz and was a rich heiress who married four times, adding each time vastly to her wealth. A woman of great competence and brilliance, she was orphaned at age 9 when her father committed suicide. He had become very rich by inheritance at the age of 21 and, like so many others of the time, this excessive wealth led him on a moral slide into degeneracy. His many fierce arguments in the town eventually led to his murdering of two men, including his best friend, at the gateway of Fitzford House. He became slowly insane before finally taking his own life.

After his death King James I intervened and sold Mary to the Earl of Northumberland who forced her to marry his brother, Sir Alan Percy, when she was 12. Legend tells that she murdered her four husbands but this would seem to reflect more the fact that she was hated by proxy as being the daughter of Sir John. In point of fact, Sir Alan Percy died after catching a cold on a hunting expedition and her second husband Thomas Darcy, the only one of the four who she actually married for love, tragically died two months after the couple eloped and wed.

Both of her remaining two marriages were for money, but in later life Mary was a far more assertive character than she had been in her youth and she soon ensured that her fortune was secured so that her husbands could not exploit it. This led to bitter arguments and the break up of both marriages, with the husbands' deaths following.

The hatred and animosity towards Lady Howard is very apparent and she died hounded by all her relatives and friendless, broken-hearted following the premature death of her son George from her last marriage. It is here, in the manner of proper vengeance, that the underdogs came back at her. The events of her own life became merged with her father's and the stories of her husbands' deaths became more malicious until the legend began to take shape. It was said that every night at midnight her coach emerged from the gateway of Fitzford: on its four corners were the skulls of her four husbands, and before it ran a black greyhound with one eye in the middle of its forehead.

This striking cortege proceeded along the old road to Okehampton and is said to have been seen at Bridestow, on the road from Tavistock to Okehampton and at Lydford. At Bridestow she comes round a corner of the lane, where the Ghost-tree (an ancient and blasted oak) was named after her. If a midnight wayfarer was overtaken by it, it was said that Lady Howard would graciously offer a lift. However, since this unexpected hospitality could only have a most sinister outcome it was advised to refuse the offer. There is a report from the 19th century of a sighting of a dog pacing a stagecoach on this route. A sighting of an apparition of a dog was also made in the late 19th century by Mrs E.G. Pearse of Sticklepath. She recounted this to Fyfe Robertson of the BBC's Tonight television programme in 1960.

The story became well known and even ended up as a ballad. Although the original has long since vanished, it was reconstructed by the Rev Sabine Baring-Gould, a prolific Victorian antiquarian, novelist and scholar, from fragments that he discovered:

> *My ladye hath a sable coach,*
> *And horses two and four;*

My ladye hath a black blood-hound
That runneth on before.
My ladye's coach hath nodding plumes,
The driver hath no head;
My ladye is an ashen white,
As one that long is dead.

"Now pray step in!" my ladye saith,
"Now pray step in and ride."
I thank thee, I had rather walk
Than gather to thy side.
The wheels go round without a sound,
Or tramp or turn of wheels;
As cloud at night, in pale moonlight,
Along the carriage steals.
"Now pray step in!" my ladye saith,
"Now prithee come to me."
She takes the baby from the crib,
She sits it on her knee.
"Now pray step in!" my ladye saith,
"Now pray step in and ride."
Then deadly pale, in waving veil,
She takes to her the bride.

"Now pray step in!" my ladye saith,
"There's room I wot for you."
She wav'd her hand, the coach did stand,
The Squire within she drew.
"Now pray step in!" my ladye saith,
"Why shouldst thou trudge afoot?"
She took the gaffer in by her,
His crutches in the boot.

I'd rather walk a hundred miles,
And run by night and day,
Than have that carriage halt for me
And hear my ladye say—

"Now pray step in, and make no din,
Step in with me to ride;
There's room, I trow, by me for you,
And all the world beside."

On arrival at Okehampton Castle, Lady Howard would descend from her coach, pluck a single blade of grass from the castle mound, return to her carriage and drive home. She was to repeat this thankless task until the whole mound was cleared, which was obviously an impossible task which would take until Doomsday. Sometimes in the story, however, the carriage was dispensed with and Lady Howard herself would take the form of a great Black Hound and do the journey alone.

It will be seen later in the Chapter dedicated to Road Dogs that this legend may be imposed on a much older tradition of a dog ghost haunting this road. Fitzford House itself is no longer in existence, a single arched gateway being all that remains. One tale tells that at an unknown period two intruding young men who hid in the house soon after midnight one night were prevented from escaping by the presence of two "very large black dogs, with eyes as big as saucers, and fiery tongues". The house was said to be have been lit up supernaturally, and at cock-crow the lights went out and the dogs vanished. It may be that these were ordinary house dogs going about their business, but were recollected in tranquillity after the event with some exaggerated terror by the guilty men.

The legend of having to carry out an endless task in death as penance for what was done in life is a common one in folklore and can also be found in one of the older Black Dog tales, which is connected to one of the four knights who murdered St Thomas à Becket at Canterbury Cathedral in 1170. All four knights had Westcountry connections: Fitzurse and Morville were Somerset men, Brito had lands in Devon and William de Tracy had a manor in North Devon at Mortehoe to which he fled after the murder. There is a surprising amount of local folklore attached to this man when we consider that he was eventually absolved from the murder and indeed was not even disgraced socially as three years after the deed he was made Steward of Normandy. However, for some reason, he alone of the four knights is credited with a 'sand-spinning' penance after death.

De Tracy is said to haunt Woolacombe Sands and Braunton Burrows spinning ropes of sand. As each attempt nears completion a Black Dog appears with a ball of fire in its mouth. With this it breaks the rope and the task recommences. Another tradition tells how the ferryman of Appledore heard someone hailing him from Braunton and rowed across. The waiting passenger turned out to be a solitary black dog, which leaped into the boat. The ferryman shrugged his shoulders and rowed back to Appledore. As they neared the shore the dog suddenly swamped the boat, jumping overboard and swimming to shore. The infuriated boatman last saw it running over Northam Burrows. It is not clear if this story has any connections to that of William de Tracy.

Family crests were not established in this period but badges were adopted on a purely personal basis. During the brief period of his disfavour, De Tracy was not allowed to sign any documents. It is said, however, that two documents of this period bore his seal which showed a hound with a very long tail.

De Tracy made many gifts to the church, a practice that was continued by his family after his death in 1174 and gave his manor at Doccombe to Canterbury. Doccombe, a hamlet near Moretonhampstead in the Dartmoor National Park, also has a Black Dog legend of its own. A shadowy form like a black dog is said to haunt a portion of the Doccombe main road. T.C. Lethbridge, again in personal correspondence with Theo Brown on 17th November 1959, says:

"It chases people up the new Exeter road as far as Cossick Cross and jumps over the road on the Exeter side of (Doccombe) at the edge of the oak scrub."

Interestingly, it appears that the name Doccombe is a corruption of 'Dog-combe'. Although this is a potentially useful piece of etymology there is no evidence that this connects to the Black Dog haunting attributed to its road. There are other instances of names in the area seeming to have some connection with the legends. Some inns in Devon have been or are named Black Dog. It takes a great deal of research, however, to discover the antiquity of such names or whether, at any time, a suitable ghost has been associated with it. An inn may be named after the whim of a new publican - after his last pub in another place, or it may be the crest of a local family. After he has gone, nobody remembers the reason.

There are two hamlets, in the parish of Washford Pyne, named Upper and Lower Black Dog. They are not very old hamlets and the area was originally open heath. At one point four roads met by a well known and old pub, which is still known as the Black Dog. It had that name on Donne's map of 1765, but about 1809 it changed its name to Black Boy. In 1813 it reverted to Black Dog, apparently to please a local squire who employed a black retriever in shooting over the heath. There is a local tradition that there was once a tunnel leading from the crossroads to an earthworks called Berry Castle. The entrance to this tunnel was guarded by a black dog at the time of the Civil Wars. None of this makes any sense historically, but folkloristically it indicates some possible communication between these two points in, probably, prehistoric times.

The Civil Wars are the only local war that people remember, hence the anachronism - it is the folk memory of a war. Any crossroads may be said, in folklore terms, to constitute a point of contact with another world. This could be either upwards into the sky, or downwards as in this case.

That this is intended at Washford Pyne is underlined by the canine guardian.

There is a very celebrated property called The Old Black Dog at Uplyme, near Lyme Regis. The current building was erected in 1916 as a hotel and public house, replacing an earlier Inn on the site which was demolished when it became unsafe. It is very close to the county boundary between Devon and Dorset but is not associated with it, and the whole complex of legends is sited in Devon, not Dorset.

The older building was listed as 'The Black Dog Inn' in White's Directory of 1850; it lies in a fork formed by the main road in front which is joined by Dog Lane, now known as Haye Lane, which runs up the back of the walled garden. The Inn itself was not the prime scene of the canine apparitions however - this began at some uncertain date at a cottage opposite.

Black Dogs frequently seem to recall the Civil War and invariably favour the Cavalier party, guarding their graves and their property. Lyme Regis was the scene of much activity at that period. This may in part account for the famous haunting but there is no record of how old the ghost is. It is possible that the Cavalier associations may have been added later to the original legend. It has been said that the owner of the original cottage on the site of The Old Black Dog bought the cottage opposite with money brought to him by the Black Dog, and that it was this cottage that later became the Inn.

The current Black Dog haunting is said to patrol Haye Lane, crossing the border every night at midnight, and people do claim to have seen it in relatively recent memory. Chambers' Book of Days, in 1888 recorded:

In 1856, a sober-minded woman in the lane met a black *"shaggy dog with fiery eyes"*, which grew larger as it approached, and *"made the air cold and dank as he passed"*. It went on swelling until it was as high as the trees, became like a cloud, and dispersed. Her husband with her saw only a vapour from the sea.

The earliest mention of the haunting in this area probably comes from a book called Traditions, Superstitions and Folklore, by Charles Hardwick. Published in 1872 this tells it as a Dorset story:

The lane apparently leads on the Dorset side to an ancient farmhouse, largely demolished in the Civil Wars, where the Black Dog used to keep the farmer company by his fireside until, taunted by the neighbours for tolerating it, he tried to chase the dog out. It ran upstairs to the attic and flew up through the ceiling. The farmer hit the spot where it had disappeared with a poker, and down fell a box of Charles I money.

In speaking of the Black Dog in Devon we cannot ignore The Hound of the Baskervilles because that is what comes first to the minds of most people when Black Dog ghosts are mentioned. Oddly enough, the Hound is not typical but quite exceptional to the usual run of such creatures. No family hound chases the head of the house to his death, that is quite certain, and so the Hound is not based directly upon any known prototype in Devon or elsewhere. However, the development of the legend in a fictional form is of great interest, since legends in general sometimes come to birth by a similar mental process.

The Hound of the Baskervilles was published in serial form in the Strand Magazine between August 1901 and April 1902. John Dickson Carr, in his Life of Sir Arthur Conan Doyle, tells us that in March 1901 Doyle was in a low state of health and went down to Cromer for four days, accompanied by his friend Fletcher Robinson. The weather was bad, and on the Sunday they stayed in their sitting room and Fletcher Robinson entertained Doyle with "legends of Dartmoor, the atmosphere of Dartmoor. In particular his companion's imagination was kindled by the story of a spectral hound." And so the idea for a plot was born. Fletcher Robinson's family lived at Ipplepen in South Devon. In a few days only, April 2nd, Doyle was staying at Princetown exploring the moor for himself.

He went to view Fox Tor Mire and this was to become Grimpen Mire in the story.

At some early period Doyle went to Ipplepen to stay with the Robinsons, and was met at the station by a smart young coachman called Harry Baskerville, descendent of a family that had once owned two manors locally but had fallen on hard times. Doyle was impressed by the name and asked to be allowed to adopt it. Harry Baskerville drove Doyle about to further sites, which in old age he named for a reporter. However, no hint has ever been brought as to the identity of the spectral hound apparently known to Fletcher. There are many vague stories of hounds on the edges of Dartmoor, the best known probably being that of Lady Howard already discussed.

Another possible source could be that of the legend of the Demon of Spreyton, this being located on the fringe of Dartmoor National Park, although the mention of the Black Dog in this is a relatively small part of the story. The events took place in Spreyton in 1682 and were recorded in a wonderfully named pamphlet of the time; "*A Narrative of the Demon of Spraiton. In a Letter from a Person of Quality in the County of Devon, to a Gentleman in London, with a Relation of an Apparition or Spectrum of an Ancient Gentleman of Devon who often appeared to his Son's Servant. With the Strange Actions and Discourses happening between them at divers times. As likewise, the Demon of an Ancient Woman, Wife of the Gentleman aforesaid. With unparalell'd varieties of strange Exploits performed by her: Attested under the Hands of the said Person of Quality, and likewise a Reverend Divine of the said County. With Reflections on Drollery and Atheism, and a Word to those that deny the Existence of Spirits.*"

You wonder if the contents of the pamphlet were as lengthy as the title!

In summary, the Demon of Spreyton was a series of poltergeist-type events where the second wife of Philip Furze of that Parish infested the house, tearing clothes and moving household items. Reading the full account it is obvious that the happenings were all down to the young servant, Francis Fey, who related the incident. But in the course of these events it is reported in the pamphlet that the spirit of the woman appeared in various forms, including "a dog, belching fire".

It is curious that no one enquired about the origin of Conan Doyle's Hound at the time of publication, nor can members of the Sherlock Holmes Club throw any light on the problem for certain. One member, Dr Morris Campbell, wrote a paper claiming it is the Black Dog of Hergest in Herefordshire. The family was that of Vaughan, related by marriage to the Baskervilles on an adjoining estate. However, the Hergest creature has no features in common with Doyle's Hound.

The Black Dog of Hergest is associated with "Black Vaughan" who was killed at the Battle of Banbury in 1469. There are two versions of the story. In the first, Vaughan is said to have returned and appeared in various forms such as a fly and a bull until he was exorcised. Campbell states that Vaughan upset farmers' carts and the like. He was reduced in size, stage by stage, until he could be shut in a snuff box. This was buried in the bottom of Hergest Pool in a wood, with a big stone on top, and so he was bound for a thousand years.

In the second version, Vaughan is supposed to have been accompanied in life by a demon dog. This haunts Hergest Court, and is seen before a death in the Vaughan family. Also, he inhabits a room at the top of the house and can be heard clanking his chain. He is also seen wandering, minus the chain, particularly in the vicinity of a pond, the "watering place" on the high road from Kington. The dog is supposed to have been seen by many people, according to a witness recounting in 1909.

It is said that the ghost was believed in by all the people of Kington. Citing A.R. Williams from the 1927 edition of Word-lore, Robert Tyley writes:

"A neighbour told my uncle that on a moonlight night he was crossing the Arrow by the bridge below the Court and distinctly saw a huge black hound walking in front of him, but beyond the bridge the beast was not."

The Pool was also feared. In the 1700s and earlier many awful things happened to passers-by: horses bolted and threw their riders, riders were found unconscious. Stories always told that 'something' had emerged from the Pond and chased them. Whatever it was, accidents were frequent.

There had been an enquiry into the identity of the ghost which identified it as a "Father Vaughan", of wicked life, who had lived at the Court. Thirteen priests assembled in Presteign Church to try and deal with the spirit. They formed a circle and lit candles and invoked the wicked spirit to appear. In the centre of the circle they had ready a small iron box. When the spirit came twelve of the priests fainted, and their candles were doused. One stood firm and though his candle burnt blue, he conjured the spirit into the box, which he at once locked. Then it was thrown into the Pond.

Many years later, a foreign owner of Hergest Court drained the Pond. The box was found in the sludge and opened. The same troubles as before began to happen again until a further gathering of parsons at Kington Church laid the ghost under a huge oak in the grounds of Hergest Court for sixty years.

It is tempting to ask whether the coachman, Harry Baskerville, was distantly related to the Herefordshire family. There was a real Hound of the Baskervilles, reflected in the family crest, but it was a friendly one. It does not terrorise or chase the head of its house - indeed nor does any other family dog in England. Apart from the name there is really nothing to connect the Hergest dog with the Dartmoor Baskerville hound.

There is a stronger possibility for the original of Conan Doyle's beast which was suggested by a writer in Devon and Cornwall Notes and Queries. Ipplepen, where Fletcher

Robinson lived, is not very far from Buckfastleigh, on the edge of Dartmoor. The parish runs up the great slopes northward, and these are scored by long, deep, narrow valleys, cut by the streams hurtling down to join the River Dart on the in-country. Tucked away in these remote areas are mysterious little old farms, manors and cottages. One of these is Brooke, where Richard Capel (or Cabell, spellings vary from report to report) lived and died in 1677. Local tradition credits him with a reputation not unlike that of "Black Hugo" in the novel, though no details are given. His death was said to be suitably unpleasant for a hunter of village maidens: he was chased across the moor by the whisht hounds until he dropped dead.

Another version of the story says that as he lay dying in his house, whisht hounds bayed outside. If we accept the last, then it could be seen to be a death warning as is found in many families and which we will examine in a later chapter. But if we accept the former, then this is a local story that Robinson may well have known and passed on. The equation of pack and single hound occurs commonly in folklore.

In 1972 Cecil Williamson, recognised as one of the founders of modern British witchcraft as well as being responsible for amassing much of the collection housed by the Museum of Witchcraft in Boscastle, Cornwall, visited the churchyard at Buckfastleigh. Whilst there he saw a dog which he described as being quite substantial looking, but when he tried to touch it he found that his hand passed straight through.

There is a postscript to the legend which is worth repeating. The remains of Buckfastleigh church, which was almost completely destroyed by fire in an act of vandalism in July 1992, are perched on the top of the hill overlooking the village. It is here that Squire Capel is buried outside the south door in an altar tomb. It is said that the parish were in a quandary about how to bury such an evil man in such a manner that his brutal spirit would not rise up and continue to plague them. Finally they buried him deeply with a heavy stone on his head. They piled the large altar tomb over his grave and then constructed what appears to be a symbolic prison to contain the tomb. It is solidly built, with a wide iron grill on the side facing the church, and on the opposite side is a strong wooden door with a locked keyhole. Young boys used to dare each other to walk clockwise around the building thirteen times and insert a little finger into the keyhole, which the prisoner would then gnaw at the tip. This is an example of a typical playground ghost-type game in the same vein as Bloody Mary or, following the film of the same name, Candyman.

There are, as is plain, some small parallels between the Hergest and Buckfast legends but this is not uncommon in folklore as stories develop over time and become attached to differing locations from a common root theme.

It is most likely that Conan Doyle would have used an amalgamation of information and legend to base his story on, from those cited here as well as general examples of spectral dogs such as the whisht hounds, yeth hounds and others. This is the general way in which stories develop after all, both from a fictional and from a folklore perspective.

FAMILY DOGS

The discussion about The Hound of the Baskervilles leads us neatly on to consider more widely that type of ghostly dog which appears to be connected in some way to the historical line of a particular family.

There are numerous families in Britain who are said to possess a "banshee" - a friendly apparition but one which appears when one of its family is about to die. These fetches take many forms: a White Lady, which is perhaps the most frequent; birds of various species; horsemen; spectral coaches; and even fishes and trees or plants which bring themselves to attention by abnormal behaviour. There are, of course, also many animal fetches such as hares, foxes and dogs.

Naturally, most families regard this as a private matter. It can therefore be difficult to find too much information on these traditions as those concerned may be reluctant to talk on the subject. We have already noted in Chapter 1 that there was supposed to be a family banshee connected to the Garth Heyworth family for example. Over time this tradition has become less spoken of, but it was still necessary to trace the descendants of Mrs Garth Heyworth to seek permission before including the story in this book. It would be potentially embarrassing for the living relatives of the family to disclose such information if they wished to keep it private. Some stories, however, have already been put into print previously or are in the public domain.

In The Night Side of Nature, published in 1848, Catherine Crowe cautiously quoted one such instance of a family Dog. She writes of:

> *"a family in Cornwall who are also warned on an approaching death by the apparition of a black dog, and a very curious example is quoted in which a lady, newly married into the family, and knowing nothing of the tradition, came down from the nursery to request her husband would go up and drive away a black dog that was lying on the child's bed. He went up and found the child dead."*

It is possible that this was at Harlyn, near Padstow, where there is a Black Dog attached to the Peter and later the Hellyer families. The house is very ancient and was originally built in the reign of Stephen. The hound was said to appear whenever one of the family was about to die and has two possible associations. The first of these relates to the story of Mother Ivey's curse in the area.

The Peter family were successful fishers and ran a lucrative pilchard business. On one occasion, after a good day's trade in the local market they had one crate left over. Mother Ivey, who was a witch, asked them to donate the pilchards to the starving people of Padstow but instead the family ploughed them into their field as fertiliser. Mother Ivey was incensed and laid a curse on the family such that every time the field was ploughed someone would die. The next time that the field was turned over, the family's eldest son was thrown from his horse and killed.

In the 1970s a man investigating the field with a metal detector suffered a heart attack and died. Although not ploughing by any sense of the word, the event was enough to rekindle interest in the old story and this was not abated when the foreman of a water company laying pipes there also died soon afterwards. The field is said to have remained fallow ever since. In 2014 whilst speaking on the subject of

Black Dogs and death folklore in Cornwall I was approached by a gentleman who was familiar with this story as he had been part of the construction team who were working on behalf of the water company to do these works. He added to this story the extra information that aside from the death of the company foreman (which was about a week after the ground in the field was broken) there was also a death in the family connected to the field almost immediately that the enabling works began.

An interesting postscript to this story (in folklore terms though sad in every other respect) concerns the fact that in 2008 the British politician and later Prime Minister David Cameron rented the property for a family holiday. The press naturally were very quick to pick up on the story of the curse and used it heavily as a hook for an otherwise tedious story. The following year, the disabled son of the Camerons tragically died at any early age. Once again it was of course deemed newsworthy to draw the connection between Mother Ivey's curse and this sad event. As a piece of factual reportage there is no obvious merit here. It is unlikely that the Cameron family would have been ploughing or even turning the soil in the field for any reason and hence the link to the family curse is tenuous at best. As a piece of folklore however, this link in the press is of interest as it adds to the development of the legend and in future years it will undoubtedly become more fully integrated. That is how mythology around a story is created after all.

The alternative association of the Peter/Hellyer Black Dog is to a golden statue of Our Lady which was buried hastily in Constantine churchyard by pirates driven ashore by their pursuers. The story of the Harlyn dog is quite an old one and when interviewed in 1945, members of the Hellyer family stated that the dog had not appeared to anyone then living.

Blenkinsopp Hall in Northumberland had a dog that appeared in the room of anyone about to die. The Hall stands on wooded parklands on the crest of Dryburnhaugh Hill.

The hill slopes down to Tipalt Road, and on the opposite side is Blenkinsopp Castle, itself said to be haunted by the ghost of a white lady. Built by John Blenkinsopp Coulson it is a castellated-style of a more modern house. George Kellett, in personal correspondence to Theo Brown on 4th September 1960, notes that the dog *"appears in the very chamber of death itself at the very moment of dissolution"*. In this case the dog may be more attached to the old house than to the family and this raises an important question. To what extent are such creatures attached to the geographic hearth or to the family?

The Cu Glàs (Grey Dog translated from the Gaelic) of Arisaig, in Inverness, was seen about the ruins of his home and as late as the twentieth century was said to have been seen snuffling around at the same time that a member of Clan Ranald was dying in South Africa. The legends of this dog go back much further however, as can be seen from this tale collected by "R.M.R." - an old gentleman living in Edinburgh who had a vast store of Gaelic legends:

> *"Several hundred years ago, a bog mortality occurred amongst the flocks in the neighbourhood of Morar and Arisaig. Shepherds who kept vigil failed to trace the marauders. One summer day, a crofter's wife left her baby outside her cottage in a cradle, while she went to the well to draw water - leaving her faithful collie dog with her litter of puppies, in charge.*
>
> *When the woman returned, she was horrified to find the cradle empty and the mutilated remains of her child strewn over the cottage pathway. Believing the bitch to be the culprit, her husband, on his return from work in the fields, dragged the dog into the woods, where he gouged out its eyes and beat it to death in a fit of rage and remorse, and afterwards returned and destroyed the litter.*
>
> *Shortly afterwards, to his great regret, he discovered that a large black wolf had alone been responsible for the crime. According to the local legend, a phantom hound is said to*

appear on occasions, to this date, in the woods of Arisaig, seeking revenge upon mankind.

Within recent times, visitors to the district have claimed to have encountered the terrifying apparition of a large shaggy dog with blazing blood-red eyes, while walking through the woods of Arisaig."

It is impossible to say for certain, with such an old tale taken out of any context, whether there is any basis in historical fact or whether it possibly has the marks of some kind of morality tale about not leaving your children unattended. There are certain parallels for example, with pixie stories concerning changelings (where the pixies steal a human child and replace it with one of their own). One such tale recorded tells how the mother of the storyteller had a child stolen by pixies while she was in her garden pegging out washing, with a pixie-child being left in its place. The mother was naturally devastated, but cared for the changeling as if it were her own. The pixie mother was so impressed by this that she returned the human child which enjoyed good luck for the rest of its life.

Leeds Castle, in Kent, was founded in 857AD by a Thane named Led, Chief Minister of King Ethelbert IV. It is from Led that the castle takes its name. The original building was constructed on the site of a Saxon Home, the Royal Manor. King Edward later created the Royal Castle in 1728.

A simple internet search for the history of Leeds Castle will turn up a number of references to the Black Dog that is said to haunt the location. These all follow broadly similar lines. The general story is that the phantom first began to haunt the castle after Eleanor Cobham, aunt of Henry VI was tried and found guilty of the crime of witchcraft. She was imprisoned in the castle around 1440 after which time the Black Dog started to appear. Sightings of this animal are said to be an omen of death.

However, there is a little more to it than this. The story actually requires some unpicking as this particular location has two black dogs associated with it. The first accompanies another ghost, a grey lady, who is said to haunt the castle and was seen by the housekeeper in the 1940s. But the second is of more relevance here as it is attached to the former owners of the castle, the Wykeham-Martin family. This was a family dog that portended disaster to the Wykeham-Martins. It was reported to be a gentle retriever-like dog that used to come and go and, if seen by strangers in the castle, was mistaken for a real dog.

It seems to be plausible that these two dogs may well come from the common root of the Eleanor Cobham tale. Most variations of the Leeds Castle Dog legend published describe the animal as being curly-haired and like a retriever but none of them mention the association with the sighting by the housekeeper. Unfortunately this sighting does not have a good description of the creature, but there seems to be no reason to suggest that the grey lady has any connection to the Wykeham-Martin family. It is probably the case that at some point in time the story of the Dog got translated onto the grey lady apparition but is not folkloristically connected through history in any other way.

Interestingly, although the Wykeham-Martin's banshee was said to be an omen of disaster to the family there is one recorded case where it actually saved the life of one of them. This was a female member of the Wykeham-Martin family who was sitting one day on a window bay admiring the vista across the moat when her gaze was diverted by a dog in the room. Intrigued by the unfamiliar creature she stood to follow it. As she drew close to the animal it vanished and, at the same moment, the bay window collapsed into the moat below.

When the family left the Castle in 1918 the dog left with them.

It seems fairly certain that many family dogs emigrate with their families in a similar way, as the following examples demonstrate.

Folklorist Ruth L. Tongue, writing in 1960, was told a tale by an old lady aged about eighty-five, who came of an old Somerset family and was then living in Bridgwater:

Family Dogs

"When I was a young girl I was living outside Toronto and I had to go to a farm some miles away one Autumn. There were woods on the way and I was greatly afraid, but a large black dog came with me and saw me to the door safely. When I had to return he again appeared and walked with me until I was nearly home, then he vanished."

Miss Tongue tells that one branch of her family hails from Lincolnshire, where the dogs are friendly and she believes that this accounts for this experience of a relation who was living in Yorkshire about 1930:

"The old lady was visiting a niece who was ill and who lived in a gamekeeper's cottage a mile from the main road in a lonely district. She left the bus, laden with packages, and as no one met her began a long walk through the early evening. She was worried because the locality had a bad name for attacks on lonely people, but she became aware of a large black dog keeping alongside, about ten feet away. Her fears left her and she talked to him but got no response. There was a spinney ahead she had dreaded but all through its blackness she saw the dog with her. When she came out into the open her cousin's house was quite close but the dog wouldn't come in. The cousin and her husband, the gamekeeper, had seen some rough fellows run for their lives just before the solitary figure of the old lady appeared from the spinney. There was nothing with her."

We will examine the role of Black Dogs as protectors in more detail in the next chapter.

When Mr George Kellett of Hebburn, Co Durham, was compiling his list of Tyneside friendly dogs in 1960 a relative told him about her sister's experience. This sister lived in Johannesburg.

"She had told them how she had been returning home one evening after having taken a pupil for her music lesson and she

*found that a native was following her. She hurried but so did
he and she became in rather a panic when a great black dog
trotted up and walked alongside her. This scared the native who
cleared off quickly. Shortly after, she realised that the dog had
disappeared."*

Of course these apparitions may have been local haunts
or they may have been a projection of the mind - they may
have known of the protective hounds of their own homes
which would give strength to the image employed, however
personal the immediate experience might have been.

Another family with its own Black Dog is that of the
Haynes from Crediton in Devon. A member of the Hayne
family wrote the following extracts in two letters to a resident
of nearby Black Dog Village in 1958:

*"One of the legends of our family was that a member was
mixed up in a drinking bout and wagered he'd get to a certain
toll gate at Crediton first, whether he broke his neck or not. As
his horse took off to clear the gate, a black dog ran out - the
horse fell and my ancestor did break his neck. A black dog is
supposed to haunt the Haynes.*

*Once, when my Mother and I were on a driving tour of
the West Coast, into Scotland ... at Durham a black dog
accompanied us, and when we baited the cob, my Mother ordered
some food should be put in the stable for it. I never expected
to see it again, but as we left Durham it appeared the usual
hundred yards ahead of us and was still with us till we got over
the Border - when it vanished. Well, my Mother was taken ill
at Skelmorlie on the Clyde, taken home to Liverpool where she
died. So we always said the Black Dog was a haunt."*

The first of these two extracts is an interesting tale, but
it is not unique. There are parallels in other stories of Black
Dog ghosts around the United Kingdom which have to call
its veracity into question. For example, there is a report of
a calendar ghost which is said to appear on New Year's Eve

on a road called the Sloane Track in the parish of Stourton in Wiltshire. In this case the spirit is said to be a headless horseman which is followed by a Black Dog. But again a wager is involved. The story goes that a man made a wager whilst at Wincanton marketplace that he could ride his horse home to Stourton in seven minutes. He took a rough route for speed and fell from the horse, breaking his neck. The similarity with the Haynes case is obvious. It is likely that the Haynes legend therefore is just that, a legend which possibly has no basis in fact but rather draws on what seems to be a more common folklore theme. It is possible that the wager stories grew out of some warning story to prevent people from riding unsafely. It is impossible to now trace the reason for certain.

If these hauntings really are inherited in the families concerned then the foregoing examples would seem to indicate that they are patrilineal. But it does not follow that this is true of every case.

In Professor Sidgwick's "Report on Hallucinations" published in the Proceedings of the Society of Psychical Research (Vol.X, 1894) a lady is mentioned who constantly sees yellow cats and black dogs. She stated that they were commonly experienced in her mother's family. On the next page, a Mrs Kearney stated that in 1892, when her step-father was very ill, she saw a cat which her mother also saw quite independently. The animal was wandering round the bed of the sick man who died the following day.

We may ask if these cases were due to some form of heredity. There is also a statement of a Mrs Welman who said that she saw a black dog at Norton Manor in 1887 which did not surprise her in the least as she said they were commonly seen in her mother's day. This case is also drawn from the Proceedings of the Psychical Research Society (1888/89).

Nearly every family omen that is traditional seems essentially associated with the name. At Zeal Monachorum in Devon, 'The White Bird of the Oxenhams' was said to appear to foretell a death in the family. Reports of the bird span from at least the 1630s to as late as the 19th century. About a dozen different families have a 'White Lady' associated with them and, even fictitiously, there is the omen associated with the Baskerville family in the famous Sherlock Holmes novel.

Freud, citing Frazer's Totemism and Exogamy, suggested that *"the totem is as a rule inherited through the female line, and it is possible that paternal descent may have originally left entirely out of account"* and again *"originally ... totems were inherited only through the female line"*.

This presents a curious problem. It is understandable that if physical defects such as haemophilia and colour-blindness are inherited matrilineally, then a psychic gift or a totem might be seen to do the same, but it is not so easy to understand why what to us is a patrilineal quality should sometimes be otherwise.

If society goes through the same evolution then we may expect an occasional throwback to the earlier form while, in general, the patrilineal totem represents a more advanced development. But it would be almost impossible to ascertain the facts sufficiently to formulate a theory on the matter because most people are amazingly unaware of their own family histories and have always been prone to destroying old diaries and notebooks. This means that while one moans at the lack of intimate information about any one individual, the sociological and group aspects of the family in the extended dimension of time are similarly lacking.

Heraldry should be able to be considered to give us a clue but it does not because we have no documentary evidence to show us what guided people in their initial choice of arms and crests. In any case, such history would not take us back far enough for coats of arms were not officially established and codified until the beginning of the thirteenth century and crests were not fixed until even later.

Greyhounds and talbots, sable and otherwise abound, mainly as crests. But there is no evidence that such families also have canine banshees, with the possible exception of the Baskervilles. Their crest, according to some portrays a wolf's head with a broken spear in its mouth. However, it seems more likely that this symbol has come about through changing representations of an earlier version, where the crest is topped with a wolf-hound's head with an arrow thrust through the neck. This is said to be in memory of an incident when a Baskerville in a temper with his hound threw his spear at it and killed it. Afterwards, in remorse since he was devoted to the animal, he perpetuated its memory in his crest. This could also make sense of the family motto *"Spero ut Fidelis"*, the literal translation of which is "I hope as faithful". It is possibly suggesting that the Baskerville in question hopes to be as faithful as his hound and also wishes that on future generations. Some sources suggest that this provides the origin of the famous Hound of the novel, but there seems to be little evidence for this.

A few crests do possess a very great antiquity, especially in some Scottish and Irish families - the cats of Clan Chattan and the gory hand of the O'Neills for example. In England, some of the Lethbridge family claim that their raven crest is descended directly from the Raven Banner of their Danish ancestor Ragner Lothbrok. There is no evidence to show that there is any totemic origin to these, or that they have any relation with family protectors or banshees.

Furthermore, though talbots are so common in heraldry, they are invariably shown with a rope attached to the collar, whereas family dogs are either nude or have a chain attached which is supposed to be heard clanking when the wearer is invisible. Even in a well-documented family it would take years of research to establish a connection.

Although many Irish families have banshee legends attached to them (in other forms) and a number of British families, as we have seen, have historical Black Dog motifs attached to them across the generations, we can also find some examples of familial Black Dog ghosts outside of the British Isles.

For example, in an article for the Journal of American Folklore entitled *"Folklore from Egypt"* published in 1941, Grace Partridge Smith discusses a family legend told to her by an informant Dorothy Pemberton of Eldorado, Saline County in Illinois. It should be noted that the article is not discussing Egyptian folklore – residents of Southern Illinois would refer to the area as Egypt because, in times of grain shortages in the north they would say that they were "going down to Egypt" when moving to the fertile fields to the south of the region for corn.

Ms Pemberton told that there was a family who had a tradition that a black dog would come and scratch at their door at times when someone in the family was about to die. On one occasion, according to this informant, the family heard scratching sounds and whining coming from the kitchen door and so opened a window to look outside for the source of the noises. Outside the back door they saw an enormous black dog and indeed, it followed in due course that a short time later their grandmother passed away.

Another very interesting story was told by a student in a folklore class to her teacher, Dr Genelle Moraine, who recorded it in a foreword to the book Ghost Dogs of the South. This student related that as a child she was staying at a house on a peninsula overlooking the sea near Cape Town in South Africa. Her father, a professor, was teaching at the university there and had brought his wife and daughter with him from England to stay together as a family. One afternoon the child was looking out of the window of the house while her mother was ironing in the same room. She saw an enormous black dog walk across the lawn and disappear round the corner of the house. She watched it come back and make a second and third circuit at which point she told her mother to come and have a look at the dog in the garden.

The mother crossed to the window to look at the dog, at which point she suddenly became very frightened and pulled her daughter back from the window. This also naturally then scared the girl as well, although she had no idea why her mother had reacted in this way.

Later the professor returned home from the university and his wife, telling him about the incident, began to cry which frightened the girl even more. The mother then revealed that her family back in England had a private tradition that for many generations the Black Dog would appear to a member of the family at a key time. In this case it did not presage a death in the family, but rather when some acute danger was present. Its role to the family was as a guardian and because of this the mother had instantly known that she and her daughter were in danger in some way.

The rest of the evening passed by without any further incident, but the following morning whilst having breakfast the family were listening to the news. A report came on detailing how a convicted murderer had escaped from jail the previous day but had been recaptured by the police. The criminal had told the police that he had been hiding in bushes in the garden outside a big house on the tip of the peninsula.

This story, and the role that the Black Dog played for the family involved, brings us to consider in more detail the protective element of the folkloric Black Dog.

DEAE NEHA
LENNIAE
T CALVISIVS
SECVNDINVS
OT ACTVS

PROTECTIVE DOGS

There is a general belief, when considering the image of the ghostly dog, that it is inherently evil. Portrayals in films and literature do much to foster this belief and it is therefore quite widespread these days with there being a much more pervasive sense of evil about reported sightings now than you find in older ones. Historically, television and film dealt with tamer subjects. From the penny dreadfuls through to the mid part of the twentieth century horror stories in literature dealt with different themes to the modern day. Horror films and literature have become far more prevalent, and themes such as lycanthropy, demonism and the like are not only dealt with more often, but are far more blatant.

In his book Tracking the Chupacabra which examines in detail the reports of the elusive creature blamed for mauling goats and other livestock in Mexico and beyond, Benjamin Radford suggests that sightings are more influenced by modern movies. The same may be true of reported sightings of the Black Dog in recent times. Trawling the internet on sites where people can record their 'paranormal' experiences you find many descriptions of horrific or demonic looking dogs. Similarly, where people are unaware of the folklore and are asking what possible explanations for their experience may be you find plenty of correspondents offering up the hellhound as a connection.

Modern consumers of entertainment have much more of a stomach for horror themes and may draw on these entertainments more in the decoding of the symbolism surrounding Black Dog folklore. Superstition, rather than fact, lies at the centre of these interpretations. Many Black Dog reports may be considered as symbolic but we should remember that symbols themselves are neither positive nor negative, good or evil, one thing or the other. Any symbol is morally neutral in itself. It is the social structure and belief (as we have already observed with religions) which imbues the symbol with its meaning and hence what is seen as good by one set of people will be seen as evil by their enemy. Symbols can also be adopted and their meaning changed. There are few people, for example, who would now see anything morally good in the symbol of the Nazi swastika but it is also not commonly known that before it was adopted by that party it was actually a British good luck symbol.

In its own right, the dog is usually a good and neutral animal. Its nature is to cleave to its master, guarding him and his property. A trespasser on that property, especially an uninvited one, will view the dog's attitude very differently from the owner. To an intruder the animal will appear snarling, wild-eyed or violent. The master will see it as obedient, protective and doing its duty. We may carry these two sides of the same canine coin over into the apparitional dogs and ask, therefore, not whether they are good or evil but rather whose are they? Are we on their good side as observers, or are we trespassers or intruders?

If the Black Dog appears as evil, demonic or potentially evil (and we will examine this particular breed of the apparition in the next chapter) then we as observers can consider that we are being given a warning. But, studying a massive range of accounts carefully, there is actually a relatively low percentage which may actually be considered as horrific. There are very few which are reported to have actually initiated an attack in British folklore on the subject, although in some other countries they are considered more evil and you do find more accounts of "physical" attacks. Some ghostly dogs are said to have retaliated when their observers have tried to beat them off with a stick or other object. But is this not in the nature of any dog?

In Hatfield Peverel, Essex, a ghostly dog known as "Shaen's Shaggy Dog" was said to walk between the two gates of a house occupied between 1770 and 1856 by the Shaen family. It was a friendly dog unless it was annoyed, at which it was supposed to emit fire. One story tells that a man driving a two-horse timber wain struck at it with a whip. The man, wagon horses and load were all reduced to ashes. We are fortunate, at least, that real flesh and blood dogs do not do the same thing!

A large number of accounts of Black Dogs are really quite neutral and comparable with the nature and characteristics of actual dogs. There may be many cases where people are scared by them, but we cannot always consider this to be the fault of the dog. In actual reports of sightings (as distinct from the more vague traditions) the helpful, protective dog occurs just as frequently as any sinister one.

In the introduction to this book I referred briefly to Laura Christensen, an American woman who reported to me an experience with the Black Dog that she had in 2010. Her case is a good starting point. As we saw earlier, prior to getting in touch she had only recently learned that her experience was not unique. She had no knowledge of Black Dog accounts or folklore and did not even know to share her story despite wanting to. So Laura had no real preconceptions to start with. Her account, in her own words, is as follows:

"My experience happened in summer 2010. I was living and working in Yerevan, Armenia with a colleague who was also a young woman. Being an American young woman living almost-alone in Armenia, where bride-kidnapping is a culturally-accepted institution, meant we always had to be on our guard.

One day when we were walking home, we passed through the public garden that bordered our neighbourhood (a beautiful, if dangerous place) and I felt a presence behind me. I turned to look and there was this enormous black dog. He was as tall as I was, with long, luxurious fur like a mane around his head and he walked very elegantly and gracefully. At first I was frightened, because though stray dogs were extremely common in the city, I had never seen one so large nor one who would pay people enough mind to follow them directly. I turned around again and kept walking and soon my nervousness fled and I felt an overwhelming sense of calm. I can't describe it very well, except to say that the calm felt like a blanket wrapped around me from the outside, rather than something I was trying to convince myself of internally.

Immediately I thought, "Oh, this dog is protecting us. He's a Guardian," even though I'd never encountered anything like him before, the thought felt quite natural. Not ridiculous or far-fetched at all.

After that I wondered where he lived and slept because I did not see him for a while and couldn't imagine why I wouldn't have seen or heard more about such a dog wandering the neighbourhood, but by all accounts he seemed to have disappeared. But then I saw him again one day as we were walking up the open road heading for the plateau. He kept pace with us, even though he was on the other side of the street. And again the feeling I got was he was majestic, graceful, calm. He radiated this sense of peacefulness and tranquility. He'd also picked up a companion, a little white dog that had much more spunk and playfulness and would frolic about, investigating this or that then coming back to the ever-noble big black dog.

After that I named him Estever, the Armenian word for Shadow, and even though I am not a dog-lover, I found myself looking forward to seeing him and feeling his peaceful sense of protection, knowing somehow that we would be safe and would not have to worry whenever he was around. We saw him again a few more times, but those first two encounters remain the clearest in my memory."

(Personal correspondence, 23 April 2014)

At first sight this appears to be an actual dog and it may well be the case. But what is interesting is the feeling that it instilled in Laura (with no conscious knowledge of anomalous Black Dogs) in an area where she would have been on her guard. It is striking, in fact, that she did not feel nervous about the dog itself after a short while when there are so many strays.

I questioned Laura on the physicalness of the dog, and she agreed that although it seemed real and physical to her she also thought that it was otherworldly. The calm and peace that it instilled equated it with the image of a *"guardian angel"* and Laura therefore considered that *"this dog was something other that was protecting us".*

There were other peculiarities in this case that mark it out as unusual even for a physical animal. Although the Black Dog walked with the two women, Laura says that she never heard it make a noise. She also described its fur as perfectly coiffed and gleaming which was unlike any other stray dog which was always matted, ruffled and dirty. Its eyes seemed kind and strangely intelligent and even though it was so big and seemed so remarkable, no one else ever stopped to watch it or talk about it.

Laura closed her answers to my questions by stating that *"most notably, the presence it had or the feeling that accompanied it ... made it clear to me that this dog was something else or had come from somewhere else, wherever and whatever that may be".*

Laura, clearly an intelligent and articulate lady, had a strong feeling about the protective nature of her dog and this has similarities to the many other examples of protective Black Dogs. Many examples of protective Black Dogs can be found across the United Kingdom but there are some areas where traditionally the apparitions tend to be seen more in this way, in the same way that other counties tend to have more menacing varieties as we shall see later.

In the north parts of Lincolnshire, for example the Black Dog is nearly always seen as a protector of travellers, especially on lonely or out-of-the-way roads. Its purpose often appears to be to guard a person against possible danger from would-be robbers or other personal threats. The folklorist Ethel Rudkin lived in this area and collected many local tales, many of which she published in a 1938 article for the journal Folklore. It would serve well at this point to look at some examples from her collection.

In 1936, whilst attending a course of lectures on local history at Kirton Lindsey, Mrs Rudkin was approached by the schoolmistress of nearby Manton. The evening had consisted of some stories of the Black Dog as part of a discussion after the lecture and the schoolmistress asked worriedly if there was any particular meaning to seeing the Black Dog. Mrs Rudkin assured the schoolmistress that in Lincolnshire there was never any harm coming from a sighting, after which the lady disclosed that she often saw one when cycling back from Manton to Kirton Lindsey. This is a trip of about three miles.

The schoolmistress told that she would often become aware of a large dog trotting along the grass verge by her side. She had never seen it disappear but generally just became aware that it was no longer there. On questioning the school children in her care, she found out that nobody in the neighbourhood owned such a large dog and so there were no clues as to where it came from. The schoolmistress said that she liked to know that it was there, presumably because it gave her a feeling of safety. A similar story was told by a district nurse at Coningsby around the year 1909. Again she was prone to needing to do a lot of cycling to get around and she too was often paced by a friendly black dog.

In these cases there is no immediate threat or imminent disaster which the dog is protecting the ladies from. It is more a case of providing some companionship and giving a sense of security; something which is natural for any pet dog to do. There are many more examples, however, where the Black Dog would actually seem to make an appearance purely because it knew that some danger was present and required action. A third example from Ethel Rudkin's collection illustrates this role also:

> *"Years ago, when Crosby and Scunthorpe were both villages, Mrs D's mother had gone from old Crosby to do some shopping in Scunthorpe. She was returning, and noticed that a very large dog was walking behind her; this was a strange dog to her, one she had never seen before. Presently she passed some Irish labourers, and she heard them say what they would do to the lone woman 'if that (something) dog hadn't been with her'. She arrived home safely and called to her husband to come and see this fine animal, but they couldn't find it anywhere – it had completely vanished."*

A similar story is recorded by the English writer and raconteur Augustus Hare in his book In My Solitary Life. He tells a tale which he hears from his friend Mr Wharton at dinner one night. Wharton acquired it from a man called Mr Bond who he met in an inn, discussing what appears to be a mutual friend Johnnie Greenwood.

"Johnnie had to ride through a wood a mile long to the place he was going to. At the entrance of the wood a large black dog joined him, and pattered along by his side. He could not make out where it came from, but it never left him, and when the wood grew so dark that he could not see it, he still heard it pattering beside him. When he emerged from the wood, the dog had disappeared, and he could not tell where it had gone to. Well, Johnnie paid his visit, and set out to return the same way. At the entrance of the wood, the dog joined him, and pattered alongside beside him as before; but it never touched him, and he never spoke to it, and again, as he emerged from the wood, it ceased to be there.

Years after, two condemned prisoners in York gaol told the chaplain that they had intended to rob and murder Johnnie that night in the wood, but that he had a large dog with him, and when they saw that, they felt that Johnnie and the dog together would be too much for them."

Of course, it is quite possible that these cases were real dogs which were identified as ghostly equivalents, rather than actual Black Dogs. In the case of Mrs D's mother and the Irish labourers this is quite possible as it was a single trip. The story told by Hare does not have enough information to be able to make full sense of it. Why would Mr Bond know about the prisoner's confessions (unless he was the chaplain, but this is not made clear)? Why do Mr Bond and Mr Wharton have a chance meeting and discuss someone who they both know? The route by which this story comes to light is somewhat circuitous. Often in folklore stories develop and one event is added to another story to embellish it. On other occasions stories get mapped onto each other and amalgamate. In this case maybe the story of the man being accompanied through the woods is quite genuine and the dog is real, but the confession of the condemned prisoners is an addition.

It would be more coincidental, though not outside the realms of possibility, that the first two of Ethel Rudkin's examples above were also flesh and blood dogs who frequented the area. Sometimes quite normal dogs, which share the same protective traits as the folkloric Black Dog, can behave in the same way and still leave a little twist in the tale to blur the boundaries.

For example, in a letter printed in the Daily Post in 1994 we hear that an informer's father-in-law lived on an isolated farm in Trefonen, Shropshire, in the early twentieth century. One autumn afternoon he walked several miles over rough country to chapel as he was a preacher. After the service on the return journey, in thick mist, he lost his way as is so easily done in these remote parts. Suddenly a large black dog appeared, wagging its tail, and led him home. His wife put the dog into a warm barn, which had no windows, and gave it some food to eat before retiring and locking the door. The final part of the story, to make you wonder, is that the dog disappeared during the night. Sadly the account just falls short of telling us whether the food was also gone, as surely a ghost would not be able to eat that?

Other cases, such as the one related by Dorothy Pemberton at the end of the last chapter, appear on face value (which is how we must treat most accounts from the perspective of folklore analysis) to be more unusual. And still others leave you in no doubt that the dog in question is not a living animal. Here are two such examples collected from the internet.

The first account, written in 2011, starts with a mother in America telling how her daughter, when aged around 8, was having nightmares about things which the mother had been seeing and which she thought were apparitions. Fast forward ten years, during which time the mother sometimes saw a shadow near her daughter's door which seemed to resemble a dog. Shortly after this, the daughter moved to a shared apartment to attend college. The second night there, a roommate walked past the daughter's closed bedroom door in order to go to the bathroom. She says that she saw a dog stand up as if it had been lying in front of the door. This made her stop and think, as nobody had a dog, and suddenly the dog was gone. Later on, someone in the next apartment reported that he had heard growling the night before even though dogs were not allowed in the apartment. So did this girl have a protective dog ghost of her own which followed her through life as she was growing up?

In the second account, from May 2014, the writer tells of a lucid dream which they had where it felt like they were being chased by something and needed to get away. They remembered jumping through doorways and running up and down stairs until in the dream they jumped onto a raised platform and suddenly jolted awake. At this point they looked to their right and about 5 inches away from their bed was a Black Dog the size of a pug barking madly. However hard the dog tried, it was not able to get any closer to the author. They said that they were not scared by this, but rather felt safe and secure. After about seven seconds the dog gave up and disappeared.

It is quite likely that in this case the phenomenon is caused by a sudden arousal from the dream state, particularly as the dream is recalled as being lucid. We will examine dream dogs and the state between rousing and sleeping later in this book.

In the last chapter we noted the story of a Black Dog at Blenkinsopp Hall in Northumberland which was supposed to presage a death in the house. The same informant who supplied Theo Brown with that story also notes that on Tyneside and up the east coast of Northumberland, the Black Dog often acts as a protector. In his correspondence he writes:

> *"A man on whose word I implicitly rely told me that one dark and rather stormy night his grandmother had to walk home along the lonely Pilot's Walk by the side of the River Tyne. Near an ill-famed spot which she approached with some trepidation, she*

> *heard the gentle patter of feet and under her hand she felt a large dog who quietly walked alongside her until she was safely home".*

On another occasion described by the same correspondent, George Kellett, the site of the protective dog is a lonely road on the south bank of the Tyne, leading towards the village of Broomley:

> *"A great personal friend of the family who, when only a girl in her teens, had a lonely walk along a road which climbed through dense woodland to her home village. One night in the gathering gloom, rather later than she could have wished, she was hurrying along when, to her alarm, she saw two disreputable tramps waiting just ahead. She hesitated, frightened and dismayed for a moment, when along in front of her there trotted a large black dog which she closely followed safely past the two men. They eyed her and the dog but did not dare to interfere. As she neared her home door, the dog was gone."*

Protective Black Dogs are often associated with roads and streams, or places of transition such as gateways or parish boundaries. However, as we also find reports of dogs with entirely different characteristics in the same sorts of location, we will treat these places separately in later chapters and examine the geographic elements in more detail there. In the two cases recorded by George Kellett above the dogs seem to be related as much to the person as to the place.

Such was the case also with James Murray, the first editor of the Oxford English Dictionary who had two encounters with Black Dogs which demonstrated their protective role. These were related by his granddaughter, K.M. Elisabeth Murray, in her biography of him published in 1977, Caught in the Web of Words.

In the book, Elisabeth Murray states that James' mother and his paternal grandmother Christina claimed to possess second sight and so it was a familiar phenomenon to him.

The later of the two encounters takes place around 1875 on a mountain which is not named. It is probable, as it is around the same time that he was on a visit to Ambleside in the Lake District, that the events take place somewhere in Cumbria, but we cannot be certain. Murray was with his children on the mountain when they suddenly became caught in a thick mist. Out of nowhere a Black Dog appeared which forced them to stop in their tracks. When the mist cleared they found themselves on the edge of a dangerous precipice, the Dog having disappeared.

The earlier event, taking place in 1872, is described in more detail and is of interest as it seems to involve not only a Black Dog apparition, but that of its owner as well. James Murray's children were quite young at the time and the family all went to Hastings where James began collecting and studying shells. He had been told that a particularly rare type of shell was found on a rock reef so he decided to head for it at low tide to investigate, leaving his wife and children on the beach. He was accompanied to the reef by a large black dog which seemed not to have an owner and attached itself to him.

After crossing a long stretch of rock, Murray found that he was cut off from the further reef. He lay down and tried to gauge the depth of the water between him and his destination when he was suddenly overcome with a feeling of being in grave danger. He hurried back to the beach without even trying to cross the channel. As he approached his wife reassured him that everything was alright because the man who was with him while he was out there had told her as he passed on the way back that Murray could get across. At this point, Murray informed his wife that there had not been any man with him on the rock. Indeed, scanning the shoreline, neither man nor dog could be seen anywhere.

James Murray had another interesting happening which seemed protective, around the same time as the mountain expedition. It did not involve a Black Dog, but seemed to call upon some other form of intervention. He had been out walking in the Lake District with only an old family hand-drawn geological map to guide him, and became very lost in a remote part of the country. It was well after dark in a mountainous area and very dangerous ground to cover with poor visibility. Finding himself in such dire straits he fell on his knees and prayed to God for guidance. When he rose he ran at once to the left, jumping across tufts of firm grass when suddenly, by pure impulse, turned back. Retracing his course he jumped the stream and ran without stopping up a slope, miraculously finding firm ground and a local guide who escorted him to the nearest habitation, from where he was able to take the road home.

We may find some other examples of seemingly divine intervention, or at the very least protection of men of God. In the April 1959 edition of The Methodist Magazine Ethel Whitaker writes about her father-in-law, the Reverend Samuel Whitaker who:

> *"was stationed in the Stroud circuit in the early half of the present century. When returning from his pastoral work late one afternoon he had to walk for some miles along a lonely lane in the country. He was a slight, short man. Just as he left the outskirts of one village he realised that there was a large black dog walking close beside him. He stopped and ordered the dog to go home but the dog remained at his side so he just had to continue his walk. Sometime later he heard footsteps approaching and in the half light he saw two men – large, brutal looking fellows – advancing towards him. When they saw the dog they stopped, scowled and passed on. When my father-in-law reached the outskirts of the next village, he found that the dog had disappeared. He made enquiries of the people in both villages all of whom he knew well, but no-one recognised the dog – nor did he ever see it again."*

An earlier similar story of a non-conformist minister being escorted past suspicious characters is described in The Life of the Rev. Robert Newton D.D by Thomas Jackson in 1855. In this case the event takes place during the political disturbances of 1819 and 1820. Again, in personal correspondence from the 1960s, a Devon resident describes another event along the same lines:

> *"My mother was not free from country superstitions although she was a devoutly God-fearing woman, with a firm faith in her God and a strong belief in the efficacy of prayer... One moonlight summer night, as a girl of sixteen or seventeen, she found herself in circumstances which necessitated a walk ... from Sampford Courtenay to Okehampton. At one particular stage of the walk – which I think passed through a belt of woodland – she became very frightened for some reason that I cannot now remember, and in her fear prayed that she might have some companion to protect her. Very soon a large black dog appeared in the wood and paced quietly by her side until she was entering the outskirts of Okehampton."*

There are many more such stories as these. Often they are moving or inspiring in their content but they do all tend to read the same way after a while. It is quite possible in a number of these cases that the dogs in question are real animals, possibly strays, out on their nocturnal travels. It is part of the dog's natural instincts to be protective and they have often been used as such. The Dalmatian, for example, was once used as a carriage dog and would run alongside a horse-drawn coach to protect its owner from highwaymen. These sorts of accounts are quite similar in the way that dog is seen to accompany or pace the traveller. We can certainly appreciate in bygone times that the person concerned might be more superstitious generally, on-edge because they are nervous of their surroundings and so may misinterpret a real animal for something more ghostly.

Dogs have also been linked to healing (which can be interpreted as another form of protection). It was said that illnesses could be transferred to dogs by taking a hair from the person suffering the ailment, placing it between two pieces of bread and butter and feeding it to a dog. The condition would then be transferred to the dog and the sufferer would quickly recover. This transference idea is known in other areas of folklore as we shall see later.

The role of dogs in healing is common in Holland where two altars have been discovered to the mother goddess Nehalennia, who is usually depicted with dogs. Many mother goddesses are often accompanied by dogs and they can represent either healing or death. In this case Nehalennia is considered a goddess of the sea and protector of seafarers who often built shrines in thanks for her protection. Other similar gods and goddesses in this regard include Diana and Aesculapius who is a god of healing.

The association with dogs and healing is quite ancient. In Mesopotamia the sitting dog was a divine symbol from 1950 – 539BCE. Various inscriptions identify it as Gula, the goddess of healing. Images of the dog were also utilised as protective amulets in Assyria and Babylon.

These protective stories are part of a more general supernatural guardian motif of course, and hence the image of the dog, with all of the protective instincts that it holds, may have been mapped onto the existing. This seems quite plausible within the wider context of dogs as guardians in folklore and mythology, both of boundaries and treasures. Motifs and archetypes do have a tendency to shift and adapt over time. This may be in a macro sense, by mapping the dog image onto general protective folklore and then following on from this on a micro level within the image. So early traditions of protective dogs would see them pacing alongside a walker. With the advent of the pedal cycle the dog would run with the rider. In Anglesey, for example, we find a story of a dog which kept ahead of a man riding his bicycle along a lane before disappearing when the man reached the intersection with the main road, as if its task ended at that point.

We still find a similar thing with motor vehicles as we shall see in the chapter on roads. In general the dog has had to get fit and speed up over time to keep pace with modern transport! Naturally there are exceptions. In a letter published in the Daily Post on 14th April 1994, George Lake of Rhos-on-Sea recalled a midwife friend who was called out to an isolated farm one night during the Second World War. People had warned her that there were German prisoners at large near the farm. As she started across the fields a large black dog appeared and, with wagging tail accompanied her to the farm. When she reached her car the animal disappeared. This one much have been too tired or lazy to pace the vehicle!

Protective dogs are found in other countries with slightly different motifs or patterns of behaviour. In Latin America the Black Dog is known as Cadejo and is similar to the British Shuck type of dog which we will examine in the next chapter. However, in some areas it is believed that there are two types of Cadejo: a black one and a white one. The black variety is more evil and dangerous while the white Cadejo is said to be female and a benevolent, protective spirit. The simile is a bit like the traditional technique of identifying heroes and villains in Wild West movies by the colour of their headgear!

As a case study by way of example, Juan Carlos often worked away from his family home until late at night. When he returned home, without fail, he would find a white dog opposite his front door which would then walk behind the shack and vanish without trace. He was told that this was a white Cadejo which protected his family while he was at work.

It is widely believed in Latin America that Cadejo is the Devil and so we can find similar themes to the Black Dog protecting people on the road but with more violent angles. A man called Reginaldo used to walk 5km to Antigua from his own neighbourhood in order to see his girlfriend. He would often return at night when the roads were dark and dangerous with many robberies and murders taking place. He often saw thieves on the road but he did not heed any of the warnings given to him by his colleagues not to walk the roads at night because he was always joined on his route by a large black dog. Because of this he was never attacked. One night he sat by the roadside due to being very drunk but he was still kept safe by the dog who sat with him. The dog would always depart when Reginaldo reached his house. When the man eventually died it was said that the devil had taken his spirit, because of the belief that the Latin American black dog was the Devil in another guise. So we can see here that there is a strong parallel with many of the protective dogs from the United Kingdom. In this example, however, we have the more demonic twist reminiscent of the Hellhound that the dog (or Devil) is protecting the traveller for its own means in the end.

There is another Latin American story revolving around drinking which has very similar themes. This one tells of a mule driver who was drinking with his employees but caught one of them pretending to drink but actually throwing the alcohol away. When challenged, the man says that he won't drink because he always sees the Cadejo when he gets drunk. His boss naturally doesn't believe him and so the man challenges him to get drunk together and see what happens. They do so and, becoming very intoxicated, end up passing out under a nearby tree. During the night the man who would not drink wakes up to see and hear a large black dog matching the description of the Cadejo. He tries to wake his boss but cannot do so and ultimately passes out again.

The following morning, when the two men finally awake, they discover that one of the mules from their pack is missing. They hunt for the animal and eventually discover it tied to a nearby tree. It turns out that a local man from the area found it in the night and put it there. He tells the two men that they are very lucky as in the night a man with a machete was on the loose, obviously mad, and attacking and killing anyone that he could find. He came across two men under a tree but left them alone because of the large and fierce looking black dog that was sat with them. The owner of the mules was said to be far more accepting of the Cadejo after this event.

These two stories are very similar in their content and have all the hallmarks of traditional folktales, or friend-of-a-friend stories drawing their themes from tradition. But should we accept that all stories of Black Dog encounters, whether protective or otherwise, stem from similar things? There are certainly many traditional stories as we have seen (and will continue to examine) where there is no eyewitness account. We noted previously that many of these older traditions, where the attributes of the dog are more extraordinary, do not have any named person associated with them as a witness and hence are representative of folktales or fairy stories. They may often stem from, or form, some kind of morality tale. But I would argue that this does not necessarily account for many of the more recent accounts which are reported to me or other researchers. The people in these accounts have nothing to gain by inventing the stories. They are often concerned or downright scared by them. In the case of protective dogs they bring a sense of calm or defuse a stressful situation. So are these people drawing on an archetype or traditional collective cultural image to project an event that they need to see or interpret for some reason? It seems quite plausible.

There are many stories where people appear to be protected by dog ghosts that they are familiar with, these being hauntings by deceased relatives coming back in the form of a dog. The bulk of these stories seem to come out of Texas, where as we noted at the beginning of this book ghostly dogs are usually white. This colouring may be representative of the manner in which these dogs appear, as they usually seem to form from white smoke. The Texas dogs are usually benign spirits and often seem to protect bereaved children.

For example, an orphaned boy was said to be guarded each night by a white dog, arriving as smoke through his bedroom window. This was said to be the ghost of his mother. Similarly there is another orphaned boy, this time an older one, who seems to have been saved by the spirit of his father in the form of a dog. The boy in question came from Dallas, but left the area to go in search of women. He spent a number of evenings in the company of a married woman whose husband worked nights. After a while, her neighbours tipped off the husband who set a trap for the boy one night by not going to work. The husband was about the grab the boy and slit his throat when a white dog with eyes like fire was said to appear. The husband collapsed unconscious (a state in which he remained for a week afterwards) and dropped the razor he was using as a weapon, which spontaneously combusted on the floor.

We can also find in Texas examples where the protective dogs are connected to healing, as we examined earlier in this chapter. There is a story of a woman and her daughter who lived together for so long that everyone questioned how the daughter would cope when her mother finally died. This of course eventually happened and the daughter began almost immediately to suffer from extreme headaches which a variety of medication would not cure. One night she went out into the yard for fresh air when a puff of smoke again heralded the arrival of a white dog. This animal had a bandage wrapped around its head which was covered in pills. The dog gestured to one of these pills with its paw. The daughter took the tablet and the headache was cured almost instantly. This animal was said to be the ghost of the mother as the bandage was made from the same material as the dress in which she was buried.

Finally, there is a story of a five year old boy who lost his mother and was raised by an old lady. Despite her trying many different foods the boy would not eat and began to starve. One night, again, smoke entered his bedroom through the window and turned into a white dog. This animal proceeded to cough-up teacakes which the boy gathered up. He ate some of these and put the rest into a sack. He would continue to eat these cakes from the sack when he was hungry, and yet the sack always remained full. The teacakes were said to be the same as those made by his late mother.

Again there are no names or dates connected with these stories and they are more akin to folk tales and legend-forming than to actual sightings of ghost dogs. But the purpose of the animal is the same. Natives of the West Indies are said to be similarly protected by ghosts of their ancestors who appear in the form of dogs.

The purpose of all of the dogs that we have examined in this chapter is to be protective in some way. In virtually any case of a Black Dog report that has meaning attached to it, then the dog's purpose will be singular such as protective or connected to a family as we have seen. There appears to be one distinct tradition of a ghost dog however which bucks this trend. This is the tradition of the Hanging Hills Black Dog, sometimes referred to as the Black Dog of West Peak. Hanging Hills is found in central Connecticut, in the United States and the dog in question is described as appearing as a short-haired dog with sad eyes. The look is a little like a spaniel. In this case the Black Dog seems to have multiple readings. The theme appears to follow a similar superstition to that ascribed to seeing magpies. In the case of the bird to see one means sorrow, to see two means joy and so on. In the case of the Hanging Hills Black Dog, the meaning varies depending on how many times you meet the animal. The legend states that if you meet it once then it is for joy, twice is for sorrow, and if you meet it a third time then you shall die.

Here the dog is said to start out as protective and, upon multiple viewings becomes an omen. This turns it into something akin to the Shuck or Barguest type of Black Dog that everyone thinks of first when considering Black Dog folklore and which we move on to examine next.

SHUCKS AND BARGUESTS

Like one that on a lonesome road
Doth walk in fear and dread,
And having once turned round walks on,
And turns no more his head;
Because he knows, a frightful fiend
Doth close behind him tread.

(The Rime of the Ancient Mariner – Samuel Taylor Coleridge)

When looking at the collected reports of Black Dog ghosts, one consideration to bear in mind is that they often look like real dogs. Were it not for certain eccentricities of behaviour they could – and often do – pass for flesh and blood animals. In many cases, as I have already suggested, they probably are real dogs that have been misidentified or seen as something else. There is however a class of ghost which sometimes appears like a dog but which is actually something quite different. It may be found anywhere, like the Black Dog, but in the United Kingdom it is grouped with great concentration in East Anglia and the North-West. It appears under such generic names as Shuck, Padfoot or Barguest depending on the region in question. Black Dogs and Barguest-type animals certainly overlap and are not always easy to distinguish, but the latter has several distinct characteristics.

Nobody would ever suppose that the Barguest type could be a real animal as it always appears monstrous in some way. In East Anglia the Shuck is generally a Black Dog haunting cliffs, fens and churchyards. The name is most likely derived from the Anglo-Saxon 'Sceocca', meaning devil. The folklorist Jennifer Westwood suggests that Shuck (or its other similar counterpart dogs Shock or Shag) comes from a description of the dog's shaggy hair. Many people consider this a less likely derivation. It is worth noting for reference here though a similarity with the Cadejo, the Latin American Black Dog with shaggy hair, goats' hooves and fiery eyes which we looked at in the last chapter. Researcher Simon Burchell points out that modern Spanish dictionaries give Cadejo a secondary meaning of "a tangled knot of hair". There is a further similarity around the fact that the traditional recurring description of a Black Dog's eyes as being "as large as saucers" extends to one of the Latin American accounts where the witness states that the dog has "eyes like tortillas". It is possible that the secondary Spanish meaning for Cadejo in a hirsute description came about from the descriptions of meetings with the Cadejo rather than vice versa.

Descriptions of the way in which the Shuck or Barguest is monstrous vary between accounts. It is sometimes said to appear as headless or on other occasions with one eye in the middle of its forehead. At Kensworth, a rural parish on the Bedfordshire-Hertfordshire border, for example, the Shuck was one of three ghosts reported on the Bury Hill footpath which runs past the medieval parish church. Bury derives from the local name for manor houses in the area. Here the Shuck appeared as a black retriever with only one eye. Writing in Rambles Around Luton in

1937, P.G. Bond reported that many of the area's older residents claimed to have seen the Shuck. As late as 1977 there is personal correspondence which says that the Black Dog was still very much believed in and everyone at a Kensworth Women's Institute meeting in 1976 knew the story.

In some areas the Shuck is said to appear in the form of other animals such as calves or horses and in Norfolk as a goat.

In North-West England the Barguest is often found on the lonely moors or in churchyards. There is much ongoing disagreement about the etymology of the name. Some suggest the derivation to be from the Germanic Bar-geist (bear-ghost) or Berg-geist (mountain-ghost). Others have put forward barn-ghost, bier-ghost or burgh-ghost (from the term for a town or city) but none of these are particularly satisfactory as they do not reflect the attributes of the creature very well.

The Barguest frequently appears without a head. In North Yorkshire it can sometimes take other forms such as a mastiff, pig, calf or large donkey. In some cases the same ghost can be seen in more than one form. A monk at Byland Abbey in North Yorkshire recorded in the fifteenth-century a ghost which transferred from the image of a crow to a dog with a chain around its neck, then into a flaming shape, a moaning goat and finally the form of a man.

A text written in the 1840s which is reproduced in Francis Bamford's Passages in the Life of a Radical in 1905 tells that in Stannicliffe, near Middleton in Lancashire the ghost may be seen as a man, a calf or a dog:

> "*Stannicliffe was frequented by a demon which was but very recently quitted his haunt. At a very old gloomy house ... situated on the brow of a hill, and looking towards Boarshaw, lived, during the Civil War, one of the Hopwood retainers, named Blondly. He would seem to have been a man of ferocious*

disposition, since his name has been handed down in traditions, the fearfulness of which time has not diminished. Several men he was said to have wantonly put to death with his own hand during those lawless periods. Ever after, until a comparatively recent date the house and premises he occupied were haunted by 'fyerin' (boggarts or apparitions) which came sometimes in the form of a calf, sometimes that of a huge black dog, and sometimes in the human form, hideous and terrible. A heavy nailed door, which was hung in such a manner that it shut with violence, would at times open of itself before a stranger, or one of the family. A dog or a calf would at times trot along the passage before a person seeking admittance: the door would open wide, the person would enter the dwelling part, but nothing was seen or heard of the mysterious appearance. At the dead of night sounds would be heard as if persons were holding a conversation in whispers, doleful cries would break forth, or a crash would resound as if every piece of crockery in the dwelling was broken, when, in the morning, everything would be found in its place.

These accounts ... were narrated to me by one who had lived in the building during many years ... and whose account was subsequently corroborated by another of the same family. It was even added and confirmed in a like manner that ... members of the family ... had seen the cream-jug or the drink bottle, move from the hearth to the hob, without any visible being touching the vessels. Other things in the house were also frequently shifted, but nothing was ever broken; and the noises, appearances and displacements at length became so little thought of, that the common observation would be, 'Oh! It's nobbut Owd Blondly' or 'T'owd lad's agate agen' ... About four years ago (the house) was pulled down, and another rebuilt on its site; since which time I have not heard of any disturbance at the place."

Some aspects of this account may put us in mind of that of the Demon of Spreyton featured in the chapter on Devon and Westcountry Dogs. There are other similar accounts of manifestations of dogs in domestic hauntings. While these are not true Shucks or Barguests they do exhibit some similar characteristics.

We may also find headless dogs and shape-shifting varieties in other countries. There is an old Germanic legend of a shape-shifting dog called the aufhocker which walks on its hind legs. In Pemiscot Country, Missouri some hunters out at night saw what they described as an enormous black dog, eight feet long and without a head. One man threw an axe at it but it passed straight through and stuck into a tree. Another headless dog was also seen in Missouri, at Braggadocio.

Returning to the more spiritual home of the Shuck and Barguest is a shape-shifting tale from Lowestoft in Suffolk where it is said that an Italian traveller once stayed. As soon as he arrived a large black dog started to be seen in the area. It was assumed that the dog belonged to the Italian but the two were never seen together. When the time came for the foreigner to leave the area he called upon a local boy whom he had befriended to go with him. When the boy refused the Italian asked him to look after the dog instead.

The boy and dog would go everywhere together. One day, when swimming in the sea with the dog the boy turned for shore but the dog prevented him from heading back, growling and snarling to drive him further out to sea. When the boy looked back he was horrified to see the face of the Italian who grinned at him and then returned to canine form and attacked the boy. Eventually a passing ship rescued the boy and the dog vanished.

East Anglian folklorist Enid Porter, who locates this story as being from Lowestoft equates the dog to the Shuck although other interpretations might place the Italian as some form of sorcerer.

A further Black Dog example from Lowestoft, reported in 1988, places the animal as a foreteller of death: a local man was in this case said to have seen a dog shortly before a fishing vessel sank with all hands.

Another variation on the Shuck and Barguest type of Black Dog ghost is the Padfoot, a term that has no doubt become more familiar since J.K Rowling adopted it as a nickname for her character Sirius Black in the Harry Potter series of stories. Black, for those who have not read the books, was able to transform himself into a Black Dog in a similar manner to the Italian sorcerer from Lowestoft. Rowling uses a lot of folklore interwoven into her stories and it will not be too difficult to also see the connection between Sirius (the Dog Star) and Black as a surname also in this case.

Many Midland Celtic names derived from the Gaelic rather than Welsh. W.P.Witcutt, referring to some of the Gaelic place names to be found in Staffordshire, believed that the term Padfoot could derive from *"badda fuath"* meaning ghost dog. However, this may be disputed as the Padfoot may be found at several places in Yorkshire also, such as in the case of the Padfoot of Wakefield or the Padfoot of Berwick, the latter of which was described in the English Dialect Dictionary as *"'T' padfoot, wi' saucer eyes, used on dark nights to come clomping and dragging a chain through Barwick town-gate"*.

The former, the Wakefield Padfoot, took various guises and shows why ghost dog may not be such a suitable derivation for the name. At Westgate it was reported to appear to be the size of a calf (one of the common sizing descriptions) but was also said to have twisted spiral horns protruding from the front of its head (certainly not a common canine description!) The eyes, as we see so often, were said to fit the standard description of being as big as saucers but in this case the coat was described as being shaggy like a bear. The creature roamed the streets with an iron chain clanking where it was secured around one leg. It was pursued by a large pack of Gabriel's Hounds. Anyone who saw the animal was said to have thought that they should have died. The last of the reports of this legendary Padfoot was recorded in the year 1766.

Gabriel's hounds are a local derivation for the familiar image of the Wild Hunt which is examined in more detail elsewhere in this book.

Another version of the Padfoot of Wakefield, perhaps the most feared version, was the 'Lanhar hede'. The name most likely comes from the area of Longerhead Lane in Wakefield which runs from Nalme Bridge to Alverthorpe and was the stomping ground of this creature. It began its route from an old well near to Alverthorpe Hall, stopped at a three-lane end with the familiar clanking of chains before traversing a stretch of road under the long garden wall of the Hall. This animal was also said to be the size of a calf but here it appeared as a monkey with a white furry coat. A look from its "glittering, blazing eyes" was said to bring misfortune.

Indeed, to see any of these Barguest types of Black Dog is invariably said to be ominous in some way. This may apply either to the witness or to someone who is close to them. If the animal catches the eye of the witness this is especially bad. To meet the Shuck head-on is the most troubling event of all, for this is said to court death within the year in many cases.

It may be believed that these are old traditions which are now dead and buried. But folklore has a way of continuing to perpetuate under the surface of everyday life because every so often a story emerges which forges the links back to the older beliefs. The Shuck is no exception to this. In a 2008 article for Paranormal Magazine, Richard Holland describes an incident reported to him as occurring to a man in a village near King's Lynn, Norfolk in 1963:

> "My wife and I had gone to bed and I was just dropping off when this deathly howling started. It was so loud and sudden, it was as if someone had turned on one of those ghetto blasters at full volume in the room. I leapt out of bed and raced across the room to turn on the light.
>
> As soon as the light went on, the sound seemed to go out of the window and then move round the side of the house, to the front

gate and then down the road, diminishing as it went. I could hear it fade way out on the marshes. It had been a terrible howling: continuous, with no up and down to it. It was unearthly.

Well, I went back to bed, not knowing what to make of it, and I was just falling asleep again when it started up again in a crescendo. Again, I put on the light and again the howling faded away out onto the marshes. The same thing happened a third time that night. My wife and I were frightened to death by it."

The next day the man in question learned that his father, who was 51 years old and had always been in good health, was taken ill unexpectedly. He sadly died three days later. The man took the howling to be a warning of his father's death, drawing the link between three lots of howling and three days of illness before death. Of course, it is quite plausible that there was a rational explanation for the howling which could have sounded quite unearthly (as he described it) if it was carried on the wind. We know that the location is close to the marshes as this is stated. But we are not judging the voracity of the claim as to whether this is paranormal or otherwise. The East Anglian Shuck is said to inhabit the marshes, and tying the event to the existing folklore continues to perpetuate the mythology of the tradition.

The Barguest-Shuck type of animal never seems to be an individual animal like the more common and realistic Black Dog ghost. It is more of a generalised bogey; an impersonal creature with no associations to humans. It haunts more lonely places and does not keep human company such as the protective animals which we have already looked at, or the dogs which frequent roads or bridges which we will see later. The Barguest or Shuck form of spectral hound has various local versions: the Padfoot above, Gytrash, Skriker, Hooter and Shag for example.

We find some of these traditional cropping up from time to time in classical, and modern literature. Thomas Hardy, who is well known for incorporating many facets of local folklore and calendar customs into his writings, includes a Black Dog in Far From The Madding Crowd, although in this case it is a more protective variant which befriends Fanny when walking at Grey's Bridge on the outskirts of Casterbridge (which he based on Dorchester in Dorset). In Jane Eyre, Charlotte Bronte makes mention of the legend of the Gytrash. As recently as 2011, author Piers Warren published a supernatural thriller called Black Shuck: The Devil's Dog where the Shuck has evolved over time and becomes a threat to the lead character. There is not a large amount of folkloric evidence to tie the Shuck directly to the Devil as we find in other countries particularly, but the title is a good hook!

In Burnley, Lancashire, the Trash or Skriker is also seen as a sign of death. Notes and Queries for the years 1850-51 carries a piece which fleshes out the creature more:

> *"It has the appearance of a large black dog, with long shaggy hair, and, as the natives express it, 'eyes as big as saucers'."*

We have of course already seen many times that it is not only the residents of Burnley who use this expression. The piece continues to describe what it considers to be the onomatopoeic derivation of its name:

> *"The name 'Trash' is given to it from the peculiar noise made by its feet when passing along, resembling that of a heavy shoe in a miry road. The second appellation is an allusion to the sound of its voice when heard by those parties who are unable to see the apparition itself."*

It is unfortunate that there is but scant detail regarding the auditory qualities of this particular dog, but we can probably assume that it refers to the unnatural howling sound which seems to accompany some similar apparitions of the Shuck or Barguest type of Dog such as the example from King's Lynn above. However, as it is quite uncommon for there to be any noise at all associated with Black Dog sightings we should consider these derivations of the name as somewhat debatable.

> *"According to the statements of parties who have seen the Trash, frequently it makes its appearance to some member of the family from which death will shortly select his victim, and at other times, to some very intimate acquaintance. Should anyone be so courageous as to follow the appearance, it usually makes its retreat with its eyes fronting the pursuer, and either sinks into the earth with a strange noise or is lost upon the slightest momentary inattention. Many have attempted to strike it with any weapon they had to hand, but although the appearance stood its ground, no material substance could ever be detected. It may be added that 'Trash' does not confine itself to churchyards, though frequently seen in such localities."*

The phenomenon of sinking into the earth is not unique to this particular type of Black Dog and we will look at this in a little more detail in a later chapter. Some other mentions of this Burnley Dog also allude to the fact that it sometimes vanished in a pool of water, or that if someone tried to chase it that it would drop at the feet of the pursuer with a strange splashing sound.

The link between Black Dogs and water, and in particular rivers, is a strong one which again we will come back to in more detail. In the meantime, it is worth noting that in the 1970s researcher Ivan Bunn, who was prolific in collecting and studying Shuck stories around Essex and East Anglia, drew correlations between these and water. Aside from more stories where the animal disappears into a pool, Bunn collected a story that said that at Blickling Hall in Norfolk the Shuck emerges from the mouth of a large fish that is caught in a lake in the area.

When owners of the Hall, Lord and Lady Lothian first moved in they decided to remove some partitions and alter the layout of the building in order to create a morning room. An old woman in the village is said to have told the local vicar that they should not do this, because of the Dog. This refers to the Shuck which emerged from the fish previously and which had become bound in the house, walking in continual circles. The previous owners had sent for a learned man from London to rid them of the curse (this is a common folklore theme). He had built the partitions in the house in order to quiet the animal. History does not record whether the Dog was seen again.

In an article published in the summer of 1977 in Lantern, Ivan Bunn notes that almost all of the Shuck stories that he has collected occur within 5 miles of water. He puts this data into a table reproduced below.

Seen within:	1 ml	2 mls	3 mls	4 mls	5 mls	5 mls +
Norfolk	26	4	3	3	-	-
Suffolk	13	4	2	-	-	-
Cabridgeshire	6	2	1	-	1	1
Essex	4	1	1	-	-	-
TOTALS	49	11	7	3	1	1

The results are certainly interesting and we will move on to examine the links between Black Dogs and water in the next chapter. We should note however that Bunn's data is somewhat limiting. While, as we shall see, there are a large number of cases where water plays an important part, this only applies to certain Black Dogs and geography also has an important part to play. Many of the traditional Shuck counties are coastal and also have many major and minor watercourses wending their way to the sea so it is natural that a high proportion of sightings can be linked to the geographical distance from water compared to more inland areas. Bunn notes that Ethel Rudkin found similar parallels to his with the Lincolnshire Black Dogs and the reasoning would carry forward to this area as well. At the time of drawing together his initial findings, Bunn was also working with a relatively small data set which does not extrapolate quite so significantly across all UK Black Dog sightings, or indeed to ones in other countries.

It has been argued that the geographic location of many of the Shuck areas means that the folklore of this Dog and its associated demeanour of being more evil than many of the other types of Black Dog is due to settlement by the Scandinavians. The premise is that the virulence of the Vikings is responsible for much of the legendary aspects of the Shuck. Danes invaded in AD869 and murdered the Angle king Edmund, proceeding to destroy the Angle monasteries. In 1014 Guthrum was appointed Norse king in East Anglia and it has been suggested that there is relevance in the fact that his nickname was "The Great Black Dog of Langport".

In this theory links are drawn between many Black Dogs being connected to water and the Viking association with the seas and oceans. It also examines the Anglo Saxon Old English language and suggests that the Vikings and Dogs may become confused in translation. For example, the Old English word for 'dog' is 'hund' which is said to be a Saxon term of abuse applied to the Vikings. Similarly, it is argued, the term 'Wulf' could mean both wolf and a cruel person and therefore it can be extrapolated that as wolf and dog are interchangeable in Old English the Vikings would have been referred to as wolves or dogs. They were also known as "wolves of slaughter" and wore wolf coats in battle as well as allegedly breeding large war dogs.

It is also suggested that elements of Scandinavian doglore would have entered the folklore of Britain at the time, such as the fact that the king of the Norse gods Odin kept two dogs whose names meant "greedy for the flesh of the dead". The name Shuck, as we have seen, is probably derived from the Old English term for the Devil and the Norse god Thor also had a dog named Shukr.

So the argument runs, but on closer examination it really seems to be something of a red herring. Linguistic roots inevitably go way back and there is probably little connection between Shuck and Shukr in other terms. There is little evidence that the Vikings entered into the British consciousness in such a way that over the following hundreds of years the folklore developed in this way. It is more likely that the Vikings led to more of a subconscious fear of the werewolf than the dog. The wolf is far more threatening as an animal. We have already noted the domesticated traits of the dog going back to prehistoric times and its role in human nature and it cannot realistically be argued that these are interchangeable with the wolf.

As far as the Old English language arguments go these also appear to be flawed. A 'wulf' was a term that called for respect (whether this was for good doings or bad) and for this reason it was included in many Anglo Saxon names, such as Beowulf. This would not have happened if it were a pure term of abuse. 'Hund' on the other hand was a rather more severe term and actually suggested that the person was lower than a slave. This would apply in the Anglo Saxon community as well, not just be directed to the Vikings. So the bones of this theory can largely be discounted.

The Black Dog is certainly well recognised as a piece of folklore in Denmark and it has many similarities there to the Shuck and Barguest. According to researcher Lars Thomas, writing in personal correspondence, it was generally regarded as a sign of death or disaster and was usually described as being very large with glowing red eyes, fitting in therefore with many commonly reported aspects.

It has also been reported in Denmark as dragging a chain as we have seen elsewhere. In the town of Sivested in the 19th century a Sunday School teacher met a large black dog with glowing red eyes on a hill in the town. It stared him in the face and when he told it to go it did so, dragging a bit of chain behind it.

Another Danish story has an interesting parallel with the Black Dog of Uplyme which, as we saw in Chapter 2, grew in size before dispersing. In the Danish story an old farmer was driving home from market one night when a Black Dog stuck its head into his carriage. It then proceeded to grow bigger and bigger before suddenly disappearing.

Returning to the United Kingdom Shuck-Barguest model, we can note that whereas the Black Dog is always established in one particular place, the Barguest is not limited in this way but can appear anywhere within a particular area. This is a real distinction between the two types.

There are some indications to suggest that smugglers faked Shucks of their own along both the East Anglian coast and in Kent in order to play upon the legends and frighten local people away from their illicit trade. They may, for example, have dressed up ponies to resemble the known descriptions of these large, black creatures of the otherworld. This was certainly a common practice and many other ghosts, both coastal and inland, may well have their origins in similar schemes.

For example, considering legends of phantom coaches such as the one of Lady Howard which we saw earlier, hearses were a popular form of ghost conveyance in the 19th century in the Westcountry. It has been proposed that many of these carriages were created by smugglers. The Brandy Bottle tree in Kingskerswell parish (on the Barton Hall estate) was a regular cache for smuggled spirits in a similar way to the method employed by Lizzy Newberry and her team in Thomas Hardy's story of The Distracted Preacher. In Kingskerswell the goods were conveyed from the coast in a hearse which was painted with luminous paint, as were the horses whose hooves were padded. If you can imagine that their heads were not painted then they would undoubtedly appear headless. This fake plays on existing traditions of phantom coaches for its success and drawing on the Shuck traditions worked in exactly the same way.

The author Wirt Sykes suggested that sightings of Shucks declined with smuggling and of course it is the case that the fakes would not have worked forever if there were no existing tradition to build upon in the first place. It was by playing on the fears and uncertainties of the age surrounding these traditional stories that the smugglers were able to exploit the Shuck (and other ghostly events) to their advantage.

Of course existing traditions play a part in many forms of storytelling. We have already seen how both Thomas Hardy and Charlotte Bronte drew on folklore as part of their tales. It is perhaps worth considering whether the Black Dog may have had a small part to play in Bram Stoker's Dracula as well. In this case Stoker would have been drawing on the Yorkshire Barguest type of dog for any inspiration.

In the novel, published in 1897, one of the first signs that the vampire has arrived in England is the strange behaviour of a normally quiet dog who could not be stopped from barking and howling while the funeral took place of the captain of the ship carrying the Count. The dog finally collapses. In folklore terms, the dog as an animal is said to be able to sense death (or even the Angel of Death) and this certainly could be seen to account for this strange behaviour in the story.

There is little direct evidence, but an interesting newspaper article was run in the Whitby Chronicle in 1873 - Whitby of course being the place where Dracula came ashore. In this article, under the headline *"A Ghost in Whitby: The Apparition Seen and Described"* we learn of a ghost which has been seen in the vicinity of the Court House and is the talk of the town. It appears to take on some shape-shifting qualities and is reported to have been seen in various forms including that of a black dog which "suddenly assumes the shape of a rather tall man, and from whose eyes burning red flames seem to issue". It would be nice to think that this story has a small part to play in the development of Stoker's work.

Smuggling may not necessarily have declined per se as an illicit trade, but the methods employed now have certainly changed as have the public's belief systems. Whilst Wirt

Sykes might have intimated a decline in Shuck sightings they have fortunately not disappeared altogether and people do still report what they believe to be encounters with the creature. Many Shuck stories are listed on the excellent website Shuckland (www.shuckland.co.uk) run by Mike Burgess and they also appear from time to time in other places.

Writing to the Fortean Times, Mr G.E. Thompson tells of an encounter his family had in 1996 when his daughter, who was 19 at the time, worked for a holiday site in Norfolk. One night, close to midnight, her parents had met her from a late shift to walk her back to their caravan when they all heard movements from some nearby bushes, followed by a snarl unlike anything that they had ever heard before. From the light of a nearby house they could make out the shape of a large dog:

> *"It stood there snarling, but unlike any dog we had ever heard – and we have always had dogs. To say we were nervous would have been an understatement. To cap it all, it had glowing red eyes. There was no way it could have been a trick of the light as the house lights were behind it. It stood there as we walked fearfully past. After a few yards I looked back, as the snarling had stopped. The creature was nowhere to be seen, though we had heard no sound of it moving."*

Once back at the caravan, Mr Thompson's wife came across an article in a magazine on phantom black dogs in Norfolk and he noted that the description of the Shuck in this article tallied with what they had seen. He also notes that they suffered a lot of bad luck after seeing this animal.

In 2014, whilst writing this book, there was a revival of interest in the Black Shuck after an archaeological dig turned up the skeleton of a massive dog. Although there is nothing to suggest that this was anything other than the bones of a Newfoundland, or similar breed, the newspapers had a field day printing drawings and descriptions of the Shuck and linking them to this find. This case is dealt with later in the chapter on Black Dogs in modern times.

For now we move forward from many of these stories, such as Mr Thompson's, of seeing Black Dogs on the roadside to examine in more depth the role of roads in Black Dog folklore.

ROADS AND BRIDGES

We now turn our attention to the largest single class of Black Dogs. At a conservative estimate, probably one-third of the many hundreds of sightings in my collection are associated with roads, lanes, footpaths and bridges. It is, of course, easy to suggest that as humans frequent these places more than fields, woods or river-banks then this would naturally account for the size of the group. Travellers tend to keep to pedestrian routes for ease or safety and so would naturally sight their dogs from the road. This poses the question, are dog ghosts located all over the place, waiting to be seen? Houses, for example, whether old ones or new ones built on field sites are occupied for much longer periods of time than most roads. But dogs which are seen in these are not more frequent than those seen patrolling a stretch of road or crossing from one side to the other.

As there are many stories in folklore of bridges being haunted we should ask whether the dog is associated primarily with the road or with the river. Ivan Bunn, in his research on the Black Shuck which we examined in the last chapter, noted an apparent geographic link between sightings and water. In Lincolnshire, the reports of Black Dogs seemed to be grouped around river valleys and streams. This was especially true where these water courses fed into navigable rivers which some take to suggest an origin of sea-born invaders. Some have suggested that the invasion of the Vikings did much to introduce the concept of dog ghosts to the United Kingdom but the evidence for this seems more likely to point towards wolf connections (and possibly further extrapolated into werewolf myths) rather than the Black Dog, as we have already seen.

There are, it is true, a number of cases which involve coastal stretches and are quite closely allied to the sea. Around the Portland area there was a strong superstition relating to the Row Dog. As usual it was said to have eyes as big as saucers (and fiery) and was as high as a man. At times of extreme weather around Portland Bill you would have to *"stand on a stone, out of his reach, or he may come up out of the hole (in the cavern) and seize you and drag you under the water"* according to a local woman interviewed in 1967.

The Row Dog – also known as the Roy Dog – was said to be rough and shaggy, which would match the normal description of the Shuck type of dog, although quite out of place in this area of the country. The idea of having origins in the sea would seem to be supported by the Norfolk Shuck which haunts the coast and is believed by many to have come from the water.. However, we cannot put too much store into this idea as we have already seen how the legend of the Shuck was well utilised by smugglers as a deterrent and I suspect that the Row Dog has a similar root.

When she was writing on the subject, the folklorist Theo Brown analysed the data in her collection of 250 or so Black Dogs and noted that of those connected with water courses and the like approximately ten were connected with rivers only, eight with streams, nine with ponds and five with wells. She found about ten reports with bridges in England and one in Pembroke. Extrapolating her data forwards there seems to be a suggestion that man-made roads are a more essential element than the water courses.

It is a worthwhile exercise to compare Theo Brown's data with that of one of her contemporaries from another country. The statistics from Le Rouzic's list of ghosts in the Carnac area of Brittany, which are mostly of the multiple or barguest type of dog, show that they haunt:

25 roads, paths and crossroads
5 areas by the sea-side
3 river-banks
16 or 17 streams
9 springs
5 ponds
25 bridges, or have an involvement with bridges

It is clear to see by comparison that in that small area of collection bridges are as important as open roads. Streams and areas of water generally are far more significant in these sightings than they are in the ones collected from Great Britain.

This discrepancy is very intriguing. Why should it be the case that Breton bridges are so much more haunted than the British ones? It has always been believed that the river itself is a treacherous and malevolent spirit, either drying up or flooding the surrounding land or seizing any available human and drowning them. For this reason, to actually attempt to cross a river – thus flouting it – was always considered as a very hazardous operation which should only be undertaken with the support of ritual and prayer. To take a highway over water and construct a permanent bridge was the most impertinent gesture of all and was taken to need the greatest skill and the protection of the highest numen.

An obvious example tying in the motif of the dog to rivers and flooding lies in Egypt. The origins of the cult of Anubis may be followed back to the Sumerian goddess Bau who was depicted with the head of a dog. It was during the early part of the Egyptian religious cycle that Anubis was linked with Sirius, the "dog star". Prior to being linked to

Isis, Sirius was the central point of the Egyptian calendar and it is here that we find the origin of the term "dog days" – the hot season that followed the heliacal rising of Sirius coinciding with the inundation of the Nile Delta.

Dog days were believed to be an evil time. Brady's Clavis Calendarium (1813) states that this is when *"the seas boiled, wine turned sour, dogs grew mad and all creatures became languid"*. In English areas the dates for this period vary but it may generally be considered to be around 24th July to 24th August. The Romans sacrificed a dog at the beginning of this period to appease Sirius, believing that the star was responsible for causing the weather.

Augurium (or Sacrum) Canarium is an annual moveable Roman celebration in late April or early May. This took place at the Porta Catularia of Rome – the direct translation of this being "Puppy's Gate". Manolis G. Sergis asserts in Dog Sacrifice in Ancient and Modern Greece that this name came about because "red bitches were sacrificed to appease the Dog-star, which is hostile to the corn, in order that the yellowing corn may reach maturity."

In the imperial cult of ancient Rome, the word numen referred to the guardian spirit of a living emperor, or to his divine power. The high priest of the College of Pontiffs was the Pontifex Maximus, the etymology of which literally means 'greatest bridge-builder'. Symbolically, the pontifices helped to form the bridge between the men and the gods, but the term can also be taken in a more literal sense. Major bridges in Rome had to be constructed over the Tiber which was a sacred river, considered as a deity in its own right. As such, only the highest authorities were able to disturb it with physical additions such as bridges.

There are also many Devil bridges in folklore across the world, usually with a story telling how the Devil either requested the bridge to be built or how he was summoned to assist in the construction. In the latter stories, a bargain is usually struck – as in other archaeological folklore stories where the Devil is involved. In the case of the Devil's bridges, he offers to help in the construction of the bridge in return for the soul of the first living thing to cross the bridge. There are parallels in many countries.

In Switzerland, recorded by W.J. Wintemberg in the article *"German Folk-Tales Collected in Canada"* published in the Journal of American Folklore in 1906, the Devil sent one of his imps to aid in the building of a bridge across a tributary of the Rhine to Alsace. The bargain was struck but the (human) bridge builder brought a black goat and pushed it across the bridge before a person could cross. In Britain, to take Herefordshire as one example, Jack O'Dent and the Devil built the bridge over the Monnow between Kentchurch and Grosmont overnight. Again the Devil was to claim the first over the bridge, so Jack threw a bone across and the Devil ended up with the dog that chased it over.

It is clear from these examples that rivers and bridges are folklorically very important. In England, rivers and streams often formed the parish boundary and both the adjacent parishes would do all they could to evade the expense of building the bridge. Most frequently, it ended up falling to the local monastery to do the work. Putting a bridge over a river was no light matter and we may note that chapels were often built either on the bridge or at one end so that wayfarers might return thanks for their deliverance and pray for the souls of those who had fallen victim to the flood.

At Totnes, in Devon, there was a chapel at each end of the bridge over the Dart, a river which is a notoriously savage predator. The Dart, like several other rivers in England is said to traditionally drown a victim each year and has its own grim couplet in local folklore:

> *"River of Dart, River of Dart:*
> *Every year thou claimest a heart"*

There is some evidence that bridges had foundation sacrifices performed in many parts of Europe in recent historic times. Maybe the Barguest of the Carnac bridges is the ghost of some peculiar multiple slaughter. The folklorist, the Rev Sabine Baring Gould believed that many spectres in churches and by bridges were the echoes of such rites, as also were the legends of the Devil assisting in bridge building (see the next chapter on Death folklore). In many of the Devon bridge stories, as in that of Jack O'Kent, it is a dog which is coaxed across the bridge and so we could presume that its ghost does the haunting and protecting.

To return to our English roads, a very large amount of dog ghosts are associated with these. They occur very thickly in Lincolnshire, although this is one of the areas where local folklorists have been prolific in collecting stories so we should not read too much into this statistic. Associated landmarks to fix the location are of various kinds including ponds, gates, trees and stiles, though not often buildings. Typically, the dog appears either spontaneously or coming through the hedge which is often said to crackle as it would with a real body being pushed through. The dog either crosses the road from one side to the other in front of the traveller or it patrols a section of the road. Often it will accompany the observer alongside until a particular landmark is reached, at which point it will vanish.

Road dogs seldom seem to frighten people according to the reports given. In fact, several people have commented on the animal's kindly expression. The vanishing point often seems to be near a tree although the particular species is rarely recorded so there are no clear statements to draw from this fact. Elms and ash are mentioned in a couple of accounts.

When a newer road is constructed, the dog will continue to follow the old track. At Somerby, for example, the dog goes through a wood following an ancient trade route from the Midlands to the East Coast. On Forraby Top, to the north of Caistor, the dog was seen in the High Street in 1939. This sighting is not far from the site of a pagan cemetery. At

Raventhorpe it runs along a Roman trackway and a sighting was reported in 1890.

These dogs simply appear without any apparent reason for doing so at various points on a road, and nobody has noticed any particular pattern to them. Sightings are more closely grouped in the north of the country and seem to cluster slightly along the valleys of rivers. In Devon and Cornwall, however, considerable evidence has been presented to suggest that there is some form of connection between 'runs' of apparitions which seem to be deliberate.

For example, the late Barbara Carbonell, who used to live in North Devon, discovered a rather vague ghost which she named the Black Dog of Torrington. The vagueness in this case is nothing to do with the physical appearance of the dog itself, but rather in pinning down its precise route. In the Transactions of the Devonshire Association for 1927, Mrs Carbonell suggested that the route of this dog covered a stretch of about one-and-a-half miles from Morchard Bishop to Winkleigh, between Blackditch Copse and Hobbymore Cross.

As a result of further research, it became apparent that the ghost had been seen in living memory at Copplestone Cross and at a number of points between there and Great Torrington. This is a distance of at least twenty miles as the crow flies. The sightings follow an ancient road, which deviates quite a lot from the existing ones, running very straight through several parishes and following lines and forgotten tracks. It is not known exactly how old this road is, or exactly where it ends.

Quoting her research in A Ghost Hunter's Game Book in 1958, author J. Wentworth Day also stated that besides the above it had been seen and heard in Down St Mary and on the lanes each side, in Hollocombe parish (especially on Wyke – or Week – Hill) and also on the Torrington road. Fitting with the common descriptions which we examined at the beginning of this book, it was said to be as big as a calf, with shining eyes, and at Week Hill it was said to bay "like a pack of hounds".

Barbara Carbonell first heard of this well-plotted road dog in 1923 when talking to her gardener. He told her that his father, who drove a wagon for the local mills at Copplestone, used to see the Black Dog when returning in the early morning hours from making deliveries at Torrington. Although scared at first he saw the dog often and became quite used to it. It accompanied his team of horses and he would walk alongside although he treated it with respect and never touched it or spoke to it directly.

Carbonell spent eight years after this initial discussion researching and plotting the route of this dog.

In his *"Countryside Matters"* column in the Western Morning News newspaper in 2002, Westcountry naturalist Trevor Beer investigated the same dog. Beer is well known as a big cat researcher and was contacted by a woman who said that she had seen one regularly when travelling home, always in the same place. They would slow their car down and see it disappear through a gateway.

She had originally thought that this animal was a dog, but on hearing about alleged big cats in the area they assumed that it must be that. (Some researchers believe that all historic Black Dog sightings were in fact big cats but this is extremely unlikely when you scrutinise the evidence closely.)

Beer and a colleague went out and drove the stretch of road, which lies between Crediton and Copplestone and is on the route of the Black Dog of Torrington. He reports that when they reached the spot in question a large black dog did indeed appear on the opposite side of the road and run along before disappearing into the gateway. When they examined the gateway they found that it was a five-bar gate and the dog, which was the size of a Great Dane, could not possibly have fitted through it.

An inhabitant of North Devon, however, has said that he always understood that the Black Dog of Torrington ran between Torrington and Chittlehampton. Indeed there are stories of a dog which haunts this route, but under a different name to that. One correspondent to Theo Brown, writing in 1958, stated that the Black Dog ran *"along Hudscot Plain at midnight"*. This is the dog which is supposed to continue to walk of Denys Rolle which we examined in Chapter Two.

It is possible to plot another line across Dartmoor between Roborough and Doccombe, on the east side of Moretonhampstead. In this case the sightings are entirely separate however, rather than being of a dog pacing the road, such as the example from Doccombe also cited in Chapter Two.

A significant part of this plotted line follows what is now the B3212 which runs across Dartmoor through Postbridge and Two Bridges. There are many supernatural stories attached to various locations along this route, the most famous probably being that of the 'Hairy Hands' at Postbridge – a pair of disembodied hands which were said to appear and grab the steering wheels of cars, or handlebars of motorbikes, and force the driver from the road.

Later investigations by highway authorities found that the road had a particularly dangerous camber around this area which could have been responsible for these accidents and which was subsequently altered and eased. Interestingly though, when holidaying in the area and staying in a caravan near Powder Mills, alongside the B3212, Theo Brown's mother alleged that she saw a hairy hand creeping up the outside of the caravan window one night and that it disappeared when she made the sign of the cross.

The B3212 is an old turnpike road originally called 'Carters Road'. This is not in recognition of any particular trade use but rather after the man responsible for building it. Heading towards Roborough from Doccombe the road crosses a desolate part of the North Moor, passing the well known Warren House Inn. Commonly said to be the highest or second highest inn in the United Kingdom (although actually the tenth highest) and with a fire that is alleged to never go out (also not true) the Warren House has a black dog sighting recorded from the 1920s. In personal correspondence with Theo Brown in 1960, the tale is recorded:

"...about 35 years ago, my father was passing the Warren House Inn at about 12.30am on his pony when all of a sudden he seen (sic) this big black curly dog, running alongside him. It was black and it stood about 3 feet tall. He tried to touch it but could not just get near it. It followed him about 300 yards and then it vanished."

As these sightings are, as we have just acknowledged, unconnected we need to treat this as a tentative line in any sense other than a geographic one. There is more potential evidence for lines of dogs that can be examined across the border from these in Cornwall.

For these a great debt must be paid to the folklorist and antiquarian Miss B.C. Spooner. She made her notes and sketch maps freely available to Theo Brown when she was doing her research and so we can learn much about the work that was being done in Cornwall to examine connections between sightings. Miss Spooner believed that she had plotted a continuous 'dog' line from Liskeard to Launceston, a distance of approximately fifteen miles. The dog here is called "Carrier" because the original dog was said to have accompanied a carrier every Saturday year after year over this road. He is supposed to be repeating the journey as many Saturdays after death as he did before. He appears differently at some sectors of the journey. At one place there is a noise of rattling chains and the dog appears as big as a yearling. At another he comes up on padded feet and is headless.

There is also the Black Dog at Callington, noted in Chapter Two, which runs from Mark Valley Mine through Rillamill, up Sellars and past Two Gates in Linkinhorne to Stoke Climsland.

What can we make of these strange 'runs' of dog sightings? They do not seem to coincide with any known prehistoric tracks, apart from the Liskeard-Launceston road which was an obvious trade route at all times. This dog accompanied a carrier as we have seen, which fits an idea that many of the road dogs might be ghosts of creatures that ran with carriers, or going back further with pack-horses and mule trains before wheeled traffic was known.

None of these routes indicated by dogs seem to link up with each other; further evidence may produce connecting runs, for example, between Stoke Climsland and Tavistock, or between Launceston and Okehampton. That two runs meet at Torrington from Copplestone and Chittlehampton indicates a junction of some importance, by the Torridge valley. The Copplestone run goes between two 'nymet' areas.

Nymet, a form of the word Nemed, is purely Celtic in origin and means sanctuary or holy place. It occurs rarely in England except in the centre of Devon where, in an area covering 96 square miles it, or some variant, is so common that it would suggest a very important sanctuary in Pagan times. Indeed Barbara Carbonell plotted a pair of sacred forests in these nymets between which the Copplestone route goes. A Roman road from Exeter runs straight through the southernmost one to a station at North Tawton. The dog runs north of it. The other run starts just east of Chittlehampton, short of the northernmost 'nymet'.

Furthermore, it is noted that a black dog was seen beyond Great Torrington, on the main Bideford-Hatherleigh road that follows the Torridge, below the great hills on which stands the village and ruined priory of Frithelstock. This was the scene of a great medieval scandal when the monks built an unlicensed chapel containing a statue in a grove on a remote hilltop above the valley. The chapel drew a considerable following from the local parishes, many members of which worshipped there with the monks. The Bishop, believing that the statue was not of Our Lady, banned the chapel in 1351 describing the image as *"of proud disobedient Eve or of unchaste Diana, rather than the most lowly and obedient Blessed Virgin Mary"*.

*It is possible of c*ourse that the chapel was nominally in honour of Our Lady, using an ancient statue that had been locally discovered. Historian T.C. Lethbridge suggested that it was most likely a local Diana, probably called Nemetona, a Romano-Celtic woodland goddess. Were dogs associated with her as with Diana? And was there once a great cult to her honour centred on Great Torrington or Frithelstock?

Contrary to general opinion there are not many black dogs hanging around crossroads; it is sometimes nothing but a convenient landmark. It is at such a point that the Roborough Black Dog exploded close to the man he was pacing and the traveller lost his senses for a while.

At Selworthy, Somerset, there is another example where a black dog appears at the point where there was once an accident to a funeral party. Some discussion on this dog can be found in the archives of Theo Brown's personal correspondence:

> *"There seems no doubt that the Selworthy people believed that their Black Dog was the ghost of a woman. Why? Surely this must be a relic of Druidic belief in Transmigration. The coffin handle was loose. The man hammered it tight with a stone. The end of it must have gone into the dead woman's skull and let the soul out. The soul appeared as a Black Dog. The man regarded it all as a perfectly reasonable matter. 'I know all about it,' he said. What would have happened if the incident had taken place in the church yard. Would you still have had a Black Dog?"*

There seems to be no information regarding the quantity of these sightings which are associated with suicide graves or gallows sites. This factor is not usually mentioned. It is generally believed that a crossroads was chosen at the site for burying the bodies of those who took their own life, or for executions, because the ghost of the departed would be confused and unable to find their way back to haunt the living. There is also, however, a less commonly discussed theory that says that because the victim of suicide or execution is deprived holy ground, this junction affords the slight sanctity of the sign of the cross (and possibly a wayside crucifix as well).

These crossroads are frequently said to be haunted, though not usually by a black dog. For example, at Bampton in Oxfordshire there is a crossroads called Cowleave Corner where there is a suicide buried. Here a ghost used to appear as an old man and vanished in the form of a calf or sheep (which would suggest the derivation of the name). In Worcester, in the parish of Leigh, someone passing Tinker's Cross, by Gallows Lane, saw "something like a lion, with eyes as big as saucers" and there was a tradition that a tinker was buried there. It is not known whether this was as a malefactor who was hanged there or as a suicide. A yew tree once grew on the site and it was suggested that it might have grown from a stake driven through the body. This sort of suggestion, though evidentially highly unlikely, is the kind which is common in folklore terms.

Some gallows sites are, however, haunted by black dogs. In many cases these are considered to be the ghosts of criminals hanged there, but there is doubt as to whether this is the correct interpretation. Murder victims are also said to leave their shadows behind, memories of their last agony. It was the practice to hang murderers on or near the site of the crime.

At Tring in Hertfordshire such a black dog sighting is recorded in Chambers' Book of Days in 1888:

> *"Within the parish of Tring, but about three miles from the town, a poor old woman was, in 1751, drowned for suspected witchcraft. A chimney-sweep, who was the principal perpetrator of this atrocious deed, was hanged and gibbeted near the place where the murder was effected. While the gibbet stood, and long after it had disappeared, the spot was haunted by a black dog. The writer was told by the village schoolmaster, who had been 'abroad', that he himself had seen this diabolical dog. 'I was returning home,' said he, 'late at night in a gig with the person who was driving. When we came near the spot, where a portion of the gibbet had lately stood, we saw on the*

bank of the roadside, along which a ditch or narrow brook runs, a flame of fire as large as a man's hat. 'What's that?' I exclaimed. 'Hush!' said my companion all in a tremble; and suddenly pulling in his horse, made a dead stop. I then saw an immense black dog lying on the road just in front of our horse, which also appeared trembling with fright. The dog was the strangest looking creature I ever beheld. He was as big as a Newfoundland, but very gaunt, shaggy, with long ears and tail, eyes like balls of fire, and large long teeth, for he opened his mouth and seemed to grin at us. He looked more like a fiend than a dog, and I trembled as much as my companion. In a few minutes the dog disappeared, seeming to vanish like a shadow, or to sink into the earth, and we drove on over the spot where he had lain.' The same canine apparition is occasionally still witnessed at the same place or near it."

We have to question whether the dog in this case represents the miserable old woman or the savage chimney-sweep.

Records show that the chimney sweep was named Thomas Colley and the woman in question Ruth Osborne who died as a result of ducking in the village pond at Gubblecote along with her husband John.

A later example of a ghost dog encountered at a crossroads near Tring is recorded by Sheila Richards in her book Ghosts of Tring, published in 1976. This record concerns someone who, coming late from Tring station at Christmas, meets a dog "like a St Bernard". He tried to stroke the dog but his hand passes straight through it. This event took place at Grove crossroads.

The herb mandrake was called by the Germans "the little gallows man" because according to the old alchemists its root resembled a human. The plant was said to object strongly to being pulled from the ground, screaming so frightfully that it struck dead anybody within earshot. Readers of the Harry Potter series will be familiar with this image from the herbology classes which the young wizards had to attend.

Looking up Haye Lane in Uplyme, the site of a famous Black Dog tradition on the Devon/Dorset border.

Multiple reports from the early 1900s tell of a Black Dog at Hoe Benham which transformed into a donkey which stood on its hind legs.

In Jersey, the Le Tchan du Bouôlé was said to presage a storm. It is here shown on a bar sign.

Facing, top: The tomb of Richard Cabel at Buckfastleigh Old Church, constructed to keep his restless spirit at bay.

Facing, Below: The ruins of Whitby Abbey, overlooking the area where Dracula came ashore in Bram Stoker's famous story.

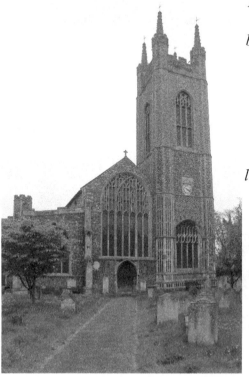

Above: The Black Dog Inn in Black Dog Village, Devon, bearing the image of a dog on its old pub sign.

Left: The Church at Bungay, site of a famous Black Dog legend in 1577 resulting in the deaths of two men

Right: Many businesses and events in Bungay celebrate the Black Dog legend in their names, and the image appears on the town weathervane

Below: The ruins of Dunwich Abbey, said to be haunted by a Black Dog ghost

The door of Blythburgh Church, showing marks above the handle said to have been left by the claws of the Black Dog which first terrorised Bungay church.

Have You Seen A Ghost?

Many everyday people have seen a ghost or thought they have. Its amazing to find out how many people have. I have seen an animal ghost which is rather uncommon.

The year was about 1974. I had been in bed a couple of hours. I awoke to hear a patter of feet. I looked up thinking it was my dog, but to my terror I saw a massive black animal probably with horns but perhaps ears galloping along the landing towards my bedroom. I tried to scream but I found it impossible. The creatures eyes were bright yellow and as big as saucers. The animal got to my bedroom door and then vanished as quick as it had appeared. I then managed to scream and my

Black Dog researcher, Dr Simon Sherwood, recorded a childhood experience which fuelled his interest in the area in a junior school book.

The old Black Dog 'oss used in the now defunct 'obby 'oss festival in Devon called 'The Running of the Black Dog.'

Image courtesy of the Pennymoor Singaround Archive.

An image from the Museum of Witchcraft & Magic's Richel collection relating to the rituals of mandrake pulling. It was said that whoever pulled a mandrake from the ground would die, and so dogs were used to obtain the magical root: "Tie the root to a dog who has been shut up and starved for three days, and show the dog food and call him – the dog will pull up the root – it will give out a cry – the dog will fall dead at the cry". Philip de Thaun, 12th century.

Folklore relates that the only way to collect the plant was to tie it to a dog (sometimes specifically a black dog) and somehow encourage the dog to pull violently and sacrifice its life in what was supposed to be a good enough cause. The botanist and herbalist John Gerarde (1545-1612) poured scorn on this fable, saying that he and his servant dug the plant up regularly in the usual way without bad effects. But for all that he quoted the saying about its origin:

> *"that it is never or very seldom to be found growing naturally but under a gallowes, where the matter that hath fallen from the dead body hath given it the shape of a man; and the matter of a woman, the substance of the female plant."*

The same story about the method of collection is told about a Palestinian herb discovered by Solomon. Its only use medicinally was for driving demons away from sick people.

There is a glimpse in classical literature which may shed some light on this herblore. The ancient goddess Hekate, often associated with crossroads and entrance-ways, was invoked as 'Hekate on the road, the black dog':

> *"the hounds with which she flies about at night are daemoniaced creatures like Hekate herself"*

A very early conception of her shows a dog's head on her and she is frequently described as appearing herself in dog form. Her terrible nocturnal howling had power only over men who had neglected to make sacrifices to her. In the train of this dark female Wild Hunt was included the ghost of Hecuba who had been transformed into a dog. So Simaethon wrote: *"Hark, the dogs are barking through the town. Hecate is at the crossroads."* At Parton Cross in Herefordshire, it is said that *"spirits in the shape of dogs are occasionally heard in the air, to terrify persons about to die."*

Many of the road dogs which we have considered so far are historical; they accompany horses and carriages or are the spirits of carriers and the like. But reports do carry forward into the more modern age where they interact with cars and other vehicles as we have briefly touched on during this chapter so far.

William Nott, a retired bus driver, recorded in the Transactions of the Devonshire Association that he was once driving his bus near Blackmoor Gate on Exmoor when a black dog ran out into the road in front of him. He expected to hear and feel a thud but there was none and, on getting out to look, there was no dog to be seen. This episode happened on Christmas Eve and is interesting because both he and the passengers on the bus saw the animal run out. It is recorded elsewhere that the dog appeared to be herding three sheep which also disappeared.

Events don't just happen on minor roads. A black dog appeared in front of the car of Ivan Potter when driving the main A30 road from Exeter to Okehampton in 1969. After writing a letter to apologise to other motorists for any sudden braking, the incident prompted a string of correspondence in the local press.

Trevor Beer, who investigated the Black Dog of Torrington when researching big cats, notes some other examples which are reported to be dogs in his book The Beast of Exmoor: Fact or Legend? One of these, from October 1984, concerns a man who had seen a black animal "the size of a Great Dane" running down the road towards him in his car headlights. He says the animal was tall enough to be looking at him over the bonnet of his car and then "just went". Beer asked the man if he meant that it ran off, to which he replied:

> *"Oh no, just went like a light going out. I just couldn't see it anymore. I just couldn't see it anymore. It isn't real like an ordinary dog, I could feel the hairs on my neck standing up. I just started the car and drove off, wasn't hanging about with that thing out there."*

This feeling experienced about the dog being otherworldly or unreal mirrors that experienced by a number of the other eyewitness accounts which have already been cited in this book. It does not have to be the case that the dog has blazing eyes or two heads to appear ghostly. In this case it is quite large, but sometimes it is just enough that seeing the dog somehow out of place or unexpectedly leads to these feelings.

Another experience from the 1980s, unpublished until now as far as I am aware, shows similar traits of the dog disappearing from the road. As in the case of the Torrington Dog investigated by Trevor Beer, there seems to be nowhere for the dog to go. This case has an unusual phantom twist to its tale as well.

The event took place in 1982 at Sizewell in Suffolk, and is drawn from private correspondence in the archive of the folklorist and author Janet Bord. The writer's informant was aged 17 at the time of the incident. They were walking with a friend around the edges of the ground belonging to Sizewell Hall at dusk and ended up on a straight stretch of road. Down one side of this road was a wall (presumably part of the Hall estate) and down the other a hedge which they described as "dense and impenetrable". As the two walked along the road they noticed car headlights coming towards them. They estimated that the car was travelling at approximately 30 miles per hour. A "huge" black dog, "larger than a Great Dane" was running alongside the passenger side of the vehicle, keeping pace quite easily.

The walkers stepped back into the edge of the road to let the vehicle past. The dog disappeared from their line of sight for two or three seconds but when they looked after the car as it went down the road they realised that the dog had vanished, although there was nowhere that it could have gone. It could not have cleared the wall or got through the thick undergrowth on the other side of the road.

Although the car was only 18 inches away from them as it passed the two had not noticed either the make of the car (despite one of them being raised in the motor trade) or the driver. Sizewell Hall was a Christian Conference Centre at the time and the walkers enquired there but learned that nobody had left the hall at the time that they reportedly saw the car and the dog. The road terminated at the hall, so maybe the walkers experienced not only a phantom black dog, but a phantom car as well?

This act of disappearing is not a modern phenomenon of course and was experienced by road travellers when they tended to move about on two wheels rather than four. In the first half of the 1910s a gentleman was cycling at dusk in a lane near to Llanfechell in Anglesey when he saw a black dog a few yards ahead of him. He described it as being the size of a calf, and looking quite fierce. It followed the bicycle and, no matter what speed the gentleman rode his bike, it continued to pace him a few yards ahead. When the cyclist reached a junction in the road the dog vanished.

This report highlights some interesting points covered elsewhere for consistency. The dog is described as being the "size of a calf", already noted as an extremely common phrase in 19th and early 20th century accounts. The size description often varies depending on cultural objects that are brought to mind as we saw earlier. The accounts from the 1980s in this section have all referred to a Great Dane, for example and we have also noted how many modern reports, especially from America, compare with a wolf which would be a much more common thought in that country.

We also see a couple of examples of sightings taking place at dusk and of animals disappearing at junctions, or earlier at crossroads. Both of these are obvious boundary states, in the case of the time of day where it is transitioning between day and night and can be considered neither one thing or the other. These liminal places and times are of great significance in folklore and occur often in Black Dog sightings.

Road dogs are not specific to the United Kingdom. Like any other form of dog apparition we can find similar traits elsewhere. For example, at Warfieldsburg, Maryland, in the United States a large black dog was sighted by two men riding near Ore Bridge Mine. This took place around the year 1887 and again the time of day was around dusk. The dog passed through a fence, crossed the road and again passed through another fence on the opposite side.

This particular apparition was well known in the area and sightings were said to have taken place back to the 1820s. One of the two men was not familiar with the legend and remarked on the large size of the dog, at which point his companion told him the story of the animal. Featuring in other sightings here is one man in a wagon drawn by horse who saw a large black dog dragging a chain. This particular feature was common in stories of this animal and we see it replicated in a number of United Kingdom accounts. It is especially associated with reports from Wiltshire.

Unusually in this case the dog was said to leave footprints in the snow, although a man who tried to strike it with his whip saw it pass straight through the animal. It is rare for reports to cite any physical tracks or other remains of the dog's activity. The Black Dog of Torrington was said to be heard to knock down the corner of the schoolhouse wall at Down St Mary when it passed by, but whenever anyone looked the wall was still physically sound. It would be unusual for an apparition to actually do any physical damage in this way (discounting any alleged poltergeist activity which is a different phenomenon). There are cases in folklore where the corners of houses have been removed because they obstructed a fairy path, but the work has been done by a human agency and not by the fairies themselves.

CHURCH GRIMS AND DEATH FOLKLORE

If you questioned a number of people about the tradition of Black Dog ghosts and asked them what their first association would be, it is quite likely that the majority would link them with a portent of doom, or more specifically with death in some way. The Black Dog can indeed, as we have already seen, be an omen of death. In 1691, people sailing on an English ship to Virginia saw black dogs and black cats around them just before the ship was wrecked.

There are generally two main reasons why dogs themselves are associated with death. Firstly, it was commonly reported that dogs would howl near the house where someone was dying. This is supposed to be because the dog can actually see death approaching as well as spirits and in some cases gods that are imperceptible to humans. The dog is said to hate evil spirits. Within the Islamic religion it is believed that black dogs can see Azrael, the Angel of Death. In ancient Scandinavia it was thought that dogs could follow the movements of the sinister death-goddess Hela. This makes the dog an intermediary factor between this world and the underworld.

Shakespeare draws on this belief and uses it on a couple of occasions to presage death or misfortune…

> *"The time when screech-owls cry and ban dogs howl*
> *And spirits walk and ghosts break up their graves"*
> (Bolingbroke – 2 Henry VI)

> *"The owl shriek'd at thy birth – an evil sign;*
> *The night-crow cried, aboding luckless time;*
> *Dogs howl'd, and hideous tempests shook down trees."*
> (Henry, on Gloucester – 3 Henry VI)

A number of charms can be employed to avert the ill-effects of the dog's howling. In Staffordshire, for example, you should remove the shoe from your left foot upon hearing the dog, spit on the sole and place it on the ground bottom upwards. You should then put your foot upon the place where you sat and this will not only preserve you from harm but will also stop the howling of the dog. A similar version to this charm exists in Norfolk where you remove the same shoe and turn it to silence the dog after three turns.

The belief that dogs can sense death, or see the Angel of Death, is not just confined to foreign cultures but examples can be found closer to home. This can be demonstrated in this account from Wiltshire from the end of the 19th century:

> *"When my mother died, we had a very favourite dog, a fox terrier, who was greatly attached to her. All our persuasions would not induce him to enter her bedroom; his abject terror was so great that we gave up all attempts to coax him into the room. On the morning of her death, the dog was asleep before the kitchen fire; suddenly he jumped up with a cry and, with his*

tail between his legs, retreated under a chair, nor could we, by any persuasion or tempting, get him to come out; there he lay all day shivering with terror. After all was over, our servant, a raw specimen from the wilds of Wilts, who was the wonder and astonishment of all the London tradespeople, told me 'she knew that missus would die directly the dog behaved so strange-like, as he saw the Angel of Death come into the house, and that fritted (frightened) him."

Some of the earliest writers make mention of the howling dog foretelling death. Pausanias talks of the dogs piercing the air with a louder than usual bark prior to the destruction of the Messenians. Capitolinus mentions that howling dogs presaged the death of Maximinus.

The second canine association with a death is a somewhat cruder one. Dogs are natural scavengers and do not hesitate to eat decaying corpses in the wild wherever they may encounter them. In some areas of the world this characteristic has led to a funerary association. The ancient Egyptians noted that their cemeteries were continually invaded by desert jackals who would scratch up the shallow graves in the sand and chew the corpses. They therefore considered that the jackal sought the company of the dead and so gradually promoted it to the rank of a god in the form of Anubis, the guardian of the gate and hence a connection with graveyards and death.

In connection with death, Black Dogs can haunt graves, gallows sites, churchyards and places where terrible crimes have been committed. Some of these are quite vague. As we have already heard, Barguests and Shucks are not usually tied to one specific location, but are sometimes reported as being found near to churchyards. On the coast of Leiston, in Suffolk, for example one was sighted at midnight in a churchyard by Lady Rendlesham. In this area the dog goes by the name of the Galley Trot.

At Mow Cop in Staffordshire a police constable had a graveyard encounter with a black dog. This probably occurred in the first half of the twentieth century and is quoted by Philip R. Leese in a 1989 publication, "The Kidsgrove Boggart and the Black Dog":

> *"Police Constable Stonehouse was on duty early one moonlit morning and was riding his bike towards Mow Cop church when 'I suddenly became aware of the sounds of an animal panting and running hard towards me, as it seemed from the lower slopes of Mow Cop, when I saw a huge dog jump from the hillside with coal black skin and red eyes, its tongue hanging out and in obvious signs of distress'. He told how it ran into the churchyard, and he felt only amazement, not fear, at the sight of this animal. However when he reached the churchyard and saw that the iron gates were locked, he realised that the animal, which clearly had seemed to him to be a real one, must have gone through the gates and was therefore a ghost."*

Sometimes, however, it is more definite that the Dog is attached to a single grave in some way. In a rare variation (for the United Kingdom although quite common in Texas) where the dog ghost is white rather than black, the Rev Norman McGee, a past vicar of St Peter's Church in Stockport, Cheshire, said that there was a large 18th or 19th century tomb enclosed by railings in the churchyard. This description brings to mind similarities with the tomb of Squire Cabell in Buckfastleigh, Devon (see Chapter Two).

Tradition held that a man used to emerge from the Stockport tomb followed by a large white dog, and that together at the time of communion they would enter the church. The man would approach the altar rails and stand waiting, with his dog beside him. We should note that nobody has ever claimed to have witnessed this sight, but it was a common tradition. This goes back to a point made at the beginning of this book about the role of folklore, which is somewhat different to parapsychology or paranormal investigation. The tradition of this particular case goes back a long way. There are hundreds of other cases with common themes across the country. What would the root of all these cases be if we could trace them right back. Are they folk memories, collective or individual?

A white dog dragging chains has also been seen in the lane near Bunbury School in Cheshire and there is a well recorded case of a yellow dog at Godley Green. This was particularly attached to a house there, which has since been demolished, but there are also reports from the surrounding area. The normal description of saucer-eyes was applied to this animal but it was often mistaken for a real dog as well as a lion and sometimes a cow. Stories suggest that the dog was not real, however, as on one occasion it paced a walker who tried to hit it but found that their hand passed straight through. Unusually the dog then sped up and passed the pedestrian before turning round and keeping pace with them again, only this time walking backwards. This event took place in the 1890s, where there are also reports of a child and a lady being accompanied by the dog on separate occasions, before in the case of the latter it vanished.

There are a number of single graves outside of consecrated ground which are guarded by Black Dogs. The most interesting of these are a scattered group of Jacobite burials in North Staffordshire. After Prince Charles Edward Stuart's collapse in Derbyshire some of his followers made for Manchester and en route they fell into quarrelling and duels. At Swinscoe on the Leek to Ashbourne Road three Jacobites were ambushed and their bodies lie buried there. A Black Dog guards this spot and also at other similar sites at nearby Oxhay Farm and Hermitage Farm, the latter having been sighted in 1916.

In the West Country a number of barrows and cairns seem to be haunted by Black Dogs, including ones on the Mendips, Blackdown and Quantock Hills and Exmoor. The Wembarrow Dog was said to be seen on Exmoor by hunting people who rode too close to the cairns. There are also many examples from the Quantocks which we examined earlier.

We do not know anything about the occupants of the barrows or their history. They do not even have old traditional names, which would suggest personal names, as some of the Welsh cromlechs have. These recall greyhounds or wolf bitches. There is Lech y filiast at Pont-y-Foal in Glamorgan, Carnedd y filiast at Ysbyty, Llety'r Filiast at Llandudno and Lech y ast at Llangoedmor in Cardiganshire. It is likely that the Welsh names are personal ones, with personal totems as the early British often used canine names. It is not as likely that they are burials of actual dogs as it is only as far abroad as India that you find dogs honoured in this way as a rule.

To return to the haunted churchyards, it is interesting to note that in modern times there are still people who fear to cross a churchyard at night. We should therefore look at the Black Dog as the guardian of these areas, in the motif of the Kirkgrim, or Church Grim – Grim meaning guardian.

The well known folklorist, historian and author, the Rev Sabine Baring Gould wrote a paper on Kirkgrims in 1887 in which he suggested that animal ghosts in or around a churchyard must be the spectres of animals used as foundation sacrifices. It was believed in the past that the first burial in a churchyard must watch over the other dead and so a dog was sometimes buried instead of a human burial for this purpose. The Black Dog as a guardian may well, therefore, be a folk memory of this practice.

In an article in Fate magazine in October 1973, Gray Usher tells how he likes to believe that he met a Church Grim one afternoon in a country churchyard whilst looking to see if any Roman pottery had been brought to the surface during the digging of new graves:

> *"Sitting in the sun outside the porch was a large, smooth haired black dog. Being a dog lover I walked up the flagged path between clipped yews to have a word with him but he got up with a yawn and vanished into the porch.*
>
> *'Ah' I thought 'the Vicar's dog. The gentleman must be inside. Better introduce myself.' And followed the dog – to find that the church door was, as is usual in those days, tight locked against vandals and there was no sign of the black dog.*

I had been only a few yards away when he went into the porch and he certainly had not come out again.

I decided that 'Grim' had been telling me that he did not approve of field archaeologists hunting Roman pots on his graves and for once denied myself the pleasure of the search."

Unfortunately, the article does not give the location of this particular church.

Baring Gould noted that fifty years previous to his paper, which would have been around the 1830s, his home church was haunted by two sows, linked with a silver chain. Other neighbouring parishes had a Black Dog, as well as a calf and a white lamb. He found parallels in Scandinavian churches and accounts which appear to be authentic of animals and children on the Continent being slain to support the foundations of bridges and dams. While there was a fundamental urge in human nature to use life to support walls and bridges, as evidence of the practice can be found all over the world, it is not necessarily the case that this tallies with the churchyard foundation sacrifices or ghosts.

The use of the dog as a foundation sacrifice is not just a British phenomenon. In the Greek harbour city of Bamboula an old well close to an undisturbed tomb brought up a find of some three dozen dog skeletons. It is unclear exactly why these were placed there but they seem to be very similar to the British examples and therefore if this is the case then it would seem to suggest a ritual belief which would date back to the 13th century BCE or earlier.

There do not seem to be any records of animal bones being found under any church in the United Kingdom, although other buildings tell a different story. Some bones of a bovine origin were found in the wall of the Deanery in Exeter, Devon many years ago but the find was too ambiguous to be able to attach any form of ritual to them. If it were a form of foundation sacrifice then it would have had to be carried out in great secrecy under cover of darkness if it related to the Christian church. This fact may, of course, account for the lack of any records in the first place. As it is also the case that many early churches were replacing pagan shrines, then these pre-Christian foundations may have been supported by a sacrifice.

Church sextons used to be well known for having their own beliefs and rituals and this was especially the case in remote country churches where the trade would tend to be handed on through the family. Vicars at this time would leave the organisation of the grave digging and burial to the sextons and specialists. We find some interesting revelations into the sexton's beliefs in the collections of the Somerset folklorist Ruth Tongue.

A Somerset family told Miss Tongue when she was young that there was a belief that a cock and a dog would keep away witches and the Devil and so certain remote parishes made sure that they used both to guard their churches. There were at least three places in the area where the very old residents stated that dogs, preferably black, were buried first to guard the holy ground from the Devil. One particular churchyard was full and when the new cemetery was opened it was expected that there would be trouble from among the parishioners. However the first funeral went off without a hitch and the parson was rather relieved. He would have been more shocked if he had actually known the reason that the parish had been so accepting. Ruth Tongue's interviewee told her:

> "*Sexton he knew what did ought to be, and he done it, and never said nothing to nobody. Us all knawed what come to Farmer's black dog. Missing evermore he was. They reckoned he's runned away (back to home). No furder that Sexton — he made sure o'that.*"

There is also a sinister use of black dogs in churchyards that was known to the Somerset sextons. Dogs were held to be in opposition to witches and it was said that an ill-wisher or conjurer, or a death-bed penitent, was interred on top of a black dog.

Several gallows sites and places of execution are said to be haunted by dogs. St Andrews on Guernsey, for example, has the remains of a prison on the borders of the Fief Rahais.

Nearby is the Rue de la Bete, a lane connecting the parishes of St Pierre du Bois and St Saviour's, between La Claire Mare and Les Rouvets. This was the main highway between L'Eree and Lower St Saviour's until a coastal road was built about 80 years ago. It is said to be haunted by a black dog, reported as usual to be the size of a calf. One gentleman, Mr Vaucourt, saw it one night when driving along the road. The dog scrambled up into the cart with him and so shocked him that he died the following day. In the 1920's, something was seen in the area by a man out walking, which apparently terrified his dog.

There was also a black dog which haunted the Forest Road in the same area. This one was said to have a chain which you could hear clanking. One woman told how her father was followed one night by this animal along the St Martin's road towards the church. In this case as well as the previous one the man was so shocked that he died soon afterwards. Both of these stories can be found detailed, along with others, in the Folklore of Guernsey which was privately published in the Channel Islands in 1975. Another Guernsey Black Dog is said to haunt Clos du Valle, by the Ville Budu. This was once the slaughter house of a monastery. Although we commonly think of locations for human execution when we link hauntings to such sites, is there a reason why this should be any different? It is still a place of death and killing and so do the same folkloric rules apply?

A very unusual sounding account, purely of the legendary variety, comes from the Isle of Man and can be found in the 1852 volume of Notes and Queries. The story most probably comes from the Castletown area where a young individual reported that people used to be pulled off their horses by black dogs. They go on to say that three coffin stones were "lately dug up" and that the area has not been haunted since. These two statements occur in the same paragraph and so we have to assume that they are connected. It is not known what the original source of this legend might be. It might be the case that the dogs are connected to the graves in some way, but it is also possible that these have been translated onto the removal of the coffin stones and folklore has developed from there. In any case the story is of interest if nothing else for the fact that there appears to be some kind of rare physical interaction between the dog ghost and the person or people.

The same piece goes on to give the following account:

> *"Our woman servant told me that her father (who used to drink) and others chased a black dog, which kept howling and screaming round the town, up and as far as the gallows post; but did not dare to go beyond, and came back as fast as they could."*

We can learn two things from this paragraph. Firstly, that the person relating the story probably does not believe in its veracity, hence the inclusion of the note that the father was a drinker. Secondly, we can see that the folklore and traditions surrounding the boundary state of crossroads and gallows posts was quite strong as the party would not venture past it.

The Isle of Man is also home to the Mauthe Doog, a well reported ghost in the shape of a spaniel which haunted Peel Castle. It was said to be such a common apparition that the soldiers stationed there became quite used to it, although they were careful not to use foul language in its presence in case it turned out to be an evil spirit trying to trick them.

Although this was the common description of this apparition, a slightly different one was given in a publication called Manx Miscellany, written for the Manx Society in 1869 by William Harrison. This said that the Mauthe Doog:

> *"was large and rough, with very shaggy head; His teeth were very prominent, his eyes were very red. From one small passage out he came – his colour black and tan ... while fiercely glared his eyes."*

"The Black Dog of Newgate" was the name of an inn close to the famous prison in London which has a well known haunting story attached to it. This also lends its name to a play published in Shakespeare's time by John Day, Richard Hathaway, Wentworth Smith and "the other poete". There are no positive records of an actual ghost sighting in the vicinity; the story would appear to have a romantic rather than traditional basis. This was published in a scathing pamphlet on the prison in 1638, entitled *"The Discovery of a London Monster, called The Blacke Dogg of New-gate"*.

In the reign of Henry III there was a severe famine which affected the inmates of the jail. A scholar, suspected of witchcraft, was thrown into the prison where he was immediately eaten by the starving men and pronounced as "good meate". Subsequently a black dog appeared at night with "eyes of red and jowls that dripped with blood". It proceeded to tear the prisoners apart, others were frightened to death and the rest escaped from the jail after having killed their warders. However, the dog still hunted them down and despatched them too. Once all of the inmates who had been involved in the cannibalism were killed, the dog vanished.

Although the story is a self-contained one, the myth still perpetuates to this day. It is said that a shapeless form moves along the top of the wall along the route which ran from the prison to the gallows site, which used to be known as Deadman's Walk. When the shape appears a nauseous smell is apparent and dragging footsteps can be heard. The prison itself was demolished in 1902 and the stone used in the building of the Old Bailey which now stands on the site. People still sometimes report seeing this black mass. This is an interesting demonstration of how folklore can spread and propagate, even when the initial story has no basis in tradition.

The earliest mention of this creature, in fact, appears to be in a poem written in 1596 by Luke Hutton, who was an inmate at Newgate. The dog seems to represent guilt and especially despair, felt by the prisoners in the awful conditions there. In more modern times the term Black Dog is well recognised as a metaphor for depression – there is an institute taking its name from the phenomenon which treats clinical depression and the like. The most commonly cited root for the term Black Dog in this way was from wartime prime minister Winston Churchill, who referred to his own struggle with depression in this way. Most sources appear to acknowledge that the phrase can be traced back to the eighteenth century, although there is no specific origin mentioned. This poem of Hutton's seems to suggest a far earlier possibility for the evolution of the term.

We do, of course, need to be mindful of the fact that just because gallows sites or places of execution are associated with black dogs, this does not mean that all sightings are ghostly. A possible example of this misidentification can be found in the archives of the folklorist Ethel Rudkin. In 1938, a lady wrote the following correspondence to her:

> *"My son and I were spending a holiday in Scotland (1938) and on September 14th went to look round Stirling Castle. On coming out of the gate of the castle, we saw a large black dog which attached itself to us – to my son in particular.*
>
> *We were going to the Beheading Stone which was some distance away on a second high hill. The dog went with us.*
>
> *I found the distance tiring, and rested on the first hill while my son went on alone to the second hill, to the Beheading Stone. The dog went with him.*

When they returned to where I had been resting, we proceeded down a narrow path, single file, and the dog, in his eagerness to get to my son, almost pushed me down in passing me. We went back to the castle, and then made our way to the town, and the dog was with us at the castle, and a little distance further we remember him being with us, but never knew when he left us."

Nothing in this account seems to suggest that we should take this to be anything other than a physical animal, despite it appearing in the archive of black dog ghosts. There is a haunting attached to Stirling Castle, but no records of a historic black dog. There seems to be some physical contact when the dog pushes past the narrator, which does not suggest an apparition and there is nothing unusual about its appearance. In fact, the correspondent herself says that she *"never thought of the black dog we saw at Stirling being anything but a real live animal, until my sister-in-law from Radbourne told me of what she had read of your writing"*. It is all too easy to see how a flesh-and-blood creature can be attributed as a spirit.

It is also possible that other wild animals could be misidentified as phantom black dogs. We have already seen how some researchers consider big cats to be responsible for black dog sightings. A letter published in 1958 also describes large foxes that resembled Alsatian dogs for example. This was from Doris W. Metcalf responding to an earlier letter on the subject of 'Werewolves in Sussex'. She said that she had seen wolf-like creatures in that county before the Second World War and was under the impression that they were the last of an old line of hill foxes. Ms Metcalf saw these animals on a couple of occasions, describing them as large and grey. She believed it probable that these foxes gave rise to many of the local werewolf legends and, in fact, considered that it may be the case that they were ancestors of the wolves that used to roam the downs of the area. It is easy to imagine how an animal such as this may be misidentified, possibly as a dog at times.

Many people who assume that the Black Dog is evil and/ or connected with death will suggest that the animal has something to do with witches, or is a hell hound. There is even an assumption, that formed the basis of a study, that virtually all dog ghosts are demoniacal and those that appeared friendly only did so because the witnesses to whom they appeared had no objection to the Devil.

As we have already seen it is very uncommon for Black Dog apparitions to actually attack people. There is an account from Darlington station where the dog was said to bite a man but even in this case it left no physical mark. Most of the death-related dogs – those associated with graves, grims, ghosts of deceased people appearing in another form – are purely passive. In the case of those dogs which are said to portend death, the animal itself is a passive messenger but is blamed for the event. To consider it another way, the effects of the animal sighted are subjective and can be blamed on the superstitious nature of the person who has the encounter.

There is of course a belief in an evil ghost generally. Some dog ghosts are related to witches and some ultimately derive from ancient images of the Devil. These are distinct however from the types of eyewitness account and tradition which we are generally discussing here. Dogs may occur in witchcraft as familiars and shape-shifting guises. They may also appear to the witches themselves as the Devil or one of his demons. Since Christianity began the Devil was often used as a figure to explain any unnatural happening because he could change his appearance and obscure himself from the witness until he chose to make himself known.

An early example of the witch's familiar can be found in the case of Lady Alice Kyteler in 1324. She was accused of witchcraft at Kilkenny, Ireland and was said to possess a familiar called Robin, the son of Artis. Robin was said to appear in three forms: a cat, a three-fold black man or a shaggy black dog. There are very few details pertaining to this case to be found. The three-fold man is of interest folklorically and one must wonder if there was some knowledge about the ancient Celtic deities and mythology which ties in. Possibly Lady Alice had some knowledge of the three-fold nature of such deities.

As regards shape-shifting, witches were supposed to be able to change their own shapes to become animals. Probably the best known of these are of course the hare and the cat. Dogs, along with horses, are mentioned quite often and far less frequently, cows. There are numerous folk tales on this theme. In some cases these centre around the pursuit or persecution of witches, such as in the oft told tale of the hare that is shot with an arrow and which disappears, and the local witch or wise woman who is found at their home the next day with a wound to the same area. In other cases stories may derive from mythology where the gods disguise themselves as animals so that they can meet with earth-dwellers safely without the humans being overwhelmed by their radiance.

This manner of disguising oneself as an animal is still found in some pagan religious orders, or in cults of various kinds. In these cases the reasoning is normally to de-humanise the priest or cult leader to make them distinct from their followers in the position of office that they hold.

Going back into history and folklore it is clear in the stories that the witch, or the witchfinder, would not necessarily be certain whether an unusual animal should be considered to be a familiar, or whether they should be seen as the Devil. It is worth pointing out that whereas the descriptions from witnesses of most ghosts are as accurate as they can be, familiars always seem to be rather vague or generalised. Records from witch-hunts never describe a familiar as being "a cat" or "a dog" but rather "something like" the animal concerned. This probably means that in most cases an ordinary animal was being described in an unnatural way, or alternatively the familiar was a mere invention and there was no animal at all.

In Goudhurst in Kent, for example, in 1648 Mary Allan and her daughter were hanged for owning a black dog. There is no evidence to suggest that this was anything other than a family pet, but the local people around the area believed that it was "a wicked and evil spirit". By this, naturally, they meant that it was Mary's familiar and in the height of the witch persecution this would have been ample evidence to secure a conviction or worse.

It was often said that witches met black dogs and entered into some form of pact with them. In these cases the animals were either the Devil or they were a familiar sent by him in order to aid the witch with her dark arts. The witches themselves did not always specify black as the colour of these; the link has probably been made later.

There is an Eastern theory that suggests that any particular ghost may come from very ancient origins and may fade or become dormant until later crimes or events on the spot rejuvenate it in some way. We have already explored how some stories can get translated onto older ones, helping to change and shape the folklore surrounding the original and the premise is similar to this in many ways. The same may be true of witches and their familiars. For example, some group of witches operated in areas known for Shucks and Barguests but the groups of the two did not necessarily coincide completely. So use of the traditional image would have been employed and maybe this helped to drive on the folklore of the tradition.

Folklorist Theo Brown suggested that the image of the devil and the transformational aspects should lead a folklorist to seek some form of dog cult as the root from which many of these black dogs emerge. In her later writings on the subject she started to explore these mythologies more heavily and incorporate them into her conclusions on the Black Dog. Many of her friends were concerned that this was leading her off track and that she was losing her way with the subject. Theo admitted herself that in this case, there seemed to be no pre-Christian cults to account for the image in the United Kingdom. Whilst there is, as we have seen, plenty of mythology surrounding the image of the dog, it would probably be unwise to explore it too deeply when looking at the development of Black Dog folklore such as this book covers.

The Devil may be used sometimes as a motif to warn against un-Christian practices. At the beginning of the twentieth century it was common for young men from the village of Sixpenny Handley in Dorset to go to a nearby ruined priory on a Sunday and play cards. It was said that one Sunday a large black greyhound-type dog with saucer-eyes and no ears ran through the room and vanished into one of the walls. Some versions say that this was the Devil in disguise and it is, of course, a morality tale on the dangers of not keeping the Sabbath holy.

Very similar stories can be found in other places. At Widecombe in the Moor, on Dartmoor, for example, the Devil was said to have taken Jan Reynolds who had fallen asleep in church whilst idly playing with a pack of cards. The Devil had tied to his horse to one of the pinnacles on top of the church tower which came crashing down as he rode off and, nearby at Birch Tor, four of the cards were said to have fallen to earth and made imprints in the fields to warn people for all time of a similar thing happening to them. This is a variant, but the message is the same.

Sometimes, the connection between the Black Dog and death may not be that the former presages the latter in some way, but rather that the dog in some way avenges the death of their master. The following story would be a good example of this and is worth quoting here because it comes from an obscure old tome which means that most modern readers would never see it otherwise. The story appears in a book written by Mr Serjeant Ballantine, a lawyer, first published in 1882 and entitled Some Experiences of a Barrister's Life. The story was told by the nephew of Sir Astley Cooper, an eminent surgeon, though of course this does nothing to guarantee its veracity.

"There had been a murder, and Sir Astley was upon the scene when a man suspected of it was apprehended, and Sir Astley, being greatly interested, accompanied the officers with their prisoner to the gaol, and he and they and the accused were all in a cell, locked in together, when they noticed a little dog, which kept biting at the skirt of the prisoner's coat. This led them to examine the garment, and they found upon it traces of blood, which ultimately led to the conviction of the man. When they looked round, the dog had disappeared, although the door had never been opened. How it had got there, and how it got away, nobody could tell."

DREAMS AND VISIONS

For some, their first encounter with the Black Dog may not be in a waking state at all, but whilst asleep or in that liminal state between sleeping and being truly awake. We have already discussed the importance of liminal boundaries, things that are neither one thing nor the other (such as dusk) and similar states occur between sleeping and waking. These are known as hypnogogic and hypnopompic states and, along with sleep paralysis, may be responsible for some Black Dog sightings.

This account was published in a letter to Fortean Times magazine in September 2000 and demonstrates some common themes:

> *"For a family holiday last year, I booked an 18th century converted barn in Suffolk within the grounds of the owner's home, just 50 yards away. On the first night I was awakened by the loudest, most intense noise which I can only describe as crackling, pulsating electricity. Struggling to open my eyes, I stared into the face of a huge black dog. It lay on the bed between my husband and myself and as I looked down the king-size bed I realised its hind was almost reaching the end. The quilt was very heavy as if the weight of the enormous dog was pulling it down and I couldn't move or make a sound.*
>
> *Although it was staring directly at me, I felt no fear. What did bother me was the noise which was incredibly loud and seemed*

*not only to be coming from all around but also from within me.
I worried that if any of our three young children (asleep across
the corridor) were crying I wouldn't hear them."*

Whilst we can only guess at some of the details of this
event for the witness, it gives us some interesting clues and
common themes to think about. The weight of the dog
pulling the quilt down has very strong parallels with Old
Hag events, or with stories of the Incubus and Succubus
where a spirit sitting on the chest of the person in bed
prevents them from moving. Similarly, in this case the
author says that she could not make a noise which is similar
to the feelings of being breathless in other sleep paralysis
examples.

The letter goes on to say that the author slept well again
after this event had taken place. So we must ask ourselves
whether, in fact, she woke at all or whether it was a very
realistic dream. The loud noise that seems to accompany
the dog features heavily. Many people will have experienced
a situation where a real noise going on inside or outside
the bedroom (an alarm clock sounding or a road drill for
example) is incorporated into a dream before they wake up
and hear the actual noise. Was this a case of some external
real world noise being heard in a sleeping dream? Or was
this an example of a waking dream? An example of the
hypnopompic state – the transition between sleep and
wakefulness?

It was a similar sort of experience which kindled a
lifelong interest in Black Dog folklore for parapsychologist
and researcher Dr Simon Sherwood. He collects sightings
of Black Dogs and has written a number of articles on the
subject which he has explored since recording in a junior
school topic book a black dog encounter he had in early life.
This is what Simon wrote:

*"The year was about 1974. I had been in bed a couple of
hours. I awoke to hear a patter of feet. I looked up thinking*

it was my dog, but to my terror I saw a massive black animal probably with horns, but perhaps ears, galloping along the landing towards my bedroom. I tried to scream but I found it impossible. The creatures eyes were bright yellow and as big as saucers. The animal got to my bedroom door and then vanished as quick as it has appeared. I then managed to scream and my mum came in to calm me down. She said it was a reflection of car headlights what I thought was a ghost. I believed this until a few years later when I was reading a local paper which had an article about a haunted council house which was inhabited by a poltergeist. A variety of objects were hurled at the family's baby child. The father claimed that a black dog rushed at him and then disappeared. He also claimed that a black goat had been seen running around the house. I also thought I saw a ghostly black goat on the landing of my old house. After reading this article I was convinced that what I thought had happened a few years back had most probably happened."

It is interesting that Simon uses the phrase "as big as saucers" to describe the dog's eyes. We have seen how this phrase has cropped up so often and yet Simon, writing this aged about 10 would not be drawing on a common contemporary expression, nor one usually employed by someone approaching their teenage years.. Is there a folk memory at work here, causing this analogy to be brought to mind when thinking about the encounter?

By his own admission, hypnopompic imagery and sleep paralysis may play a part in this encounter, but Simon believes that there is possibly more to it than this, and it seems like this may be the case. At the time he was aged somewhere between 3 and 5, so the image is not one that you would necessarily expect at that age. The event also took place in Lincolnshire, a county with many Black Dog stories attached to it. So again, we should consider whether there is some kind of folk memory or motif being brought to the front of the mind somehow. There seems to be some purpose to the encounter.

The difficulty with cases that occur in these times between sleep and wakefulness of course is that it can be very difficult for both the witness and the researcher to establish with any certainty what the exact physical conditions were. Was it even certain whether or not the case was in a period of dreaming, of wakefulness, or in that transition period between the two? In an incident recorded in personal correspondence from 1983, a male witness from Newmarket in Suffolk tells of an experience he had in August of that year that took place at one of these times. He states that he had just gone to bed and turned out the light when he heard a sound which was like a dog running up the stairs in the house. He says that the animal sounded as though it were the size of an Alsatian. He heard the dog enter the room and walk round the bed to stand very close beside him. It was panting heavily and sounded loud and menacing. The witness was scared as he believed that a real dog had got into his house but after a short while when he turned on the light beside the bed there was nothing there and the sound stopped. It also became apparent that the bedroom door was still closed.

What we cannot establish with certainty here is whether the witness had literally just gone to bed and turned the light off, or whether the event took place a little while later as he was drifting off to sleep. He suggests the former but it is difficult to be sure.

Another interesting night-time case comes from Ipswich, in the same county, in the 1970s and concerns two boys, one of whom was aged about ten. The boys shared a bedroom and one night the ten year old was heard screaming in the night. The boy's father rushed into the room and the boy told him that he had seen a 'plum pudding' dog jump onto the bed. The father naturally dismissed this as a dream, but there are a couple of interesting points that follow on in this instance.

Firstly, the second boy appeared to corroborate the incident and said that he had also seen the dog as well. Although we should consider taking this with a pinch of salt, as young children are prone to invent stories for their own amusement, again we cannot be certain from the evidence available (a simple letter from the mother of the boys) whether or not this is the case. Secondly, a further interesting event happened a few weeks later. The mother was digging in the family garden when she unearthed a number of bones. She thought that the previous occupants of the house must have had a dog and on discussing this with the neighbour she was told that they had indeed owned a Dalmatian. It is not stated that this dog had died at the house, nor that it was buried in the garden if it did, but this would appear to be the implication from the letter. So should we consider that this dream, if it was a dream, was connected to this animal, or that it was some sort of residual energy or effect of the dog's time at the house.

We have examined a number of cases in previous chapters where dog ghosts appear to be connected to their owners. These are usually connected to roads and historic routes of travel. But there can be times where this is not the case. In another account from 1977 a witness, who at the time was living in America, was visiting her retired parents in Thetford, Norfolk, for a few months. One night shortly after she had arrived she was woken to see a man standing above her with a black dog sitting next to him. She said that he was aged between 30 and 35 and looked at her in a menacing way. The dog seemed to be about the size of a Labrador and appeared to be friendly. It looked around the room but never directly at her. The woman jumped up screaming from the bed and ran downstairs where she spent the rest of the night. The man and dog were not seen again after this, either my herself or anyone else in the house.

This would lead us to suspect that in this case it is most likely that the witness dreamt the event. But we should consider whether the content of the dream was purely random, or whether the appearance of the black dog draws on any kind of folk memory. The dog appears to be quite natural and so it is far from clear.

The Native American Indians have a belief in a personal fetch, this being a totem which is artificially brought into being when a child reaches adolescence in order that the boy may benefit from its support. A totem is a being or symbol which can represent either animal or plant and becomes an emblem which links a group to their ancestry.

In Western culture we have no real appreciation of this part of our subconscious makeup and so, if people who are ill or alone, or possibly have some other anxiety, begin to have visions in this way they are deemed to be hallucinations. These can of course be very frightening for the person involved.

The artist Paul Nash, who died in 1946, recorded having a horrifying recurring dream as a small boy where he would be climbing the stairs in his house to get to the nursery. The further up the stairs he went the more uneasy he became until he reached a dark turn in the staircase. He knew that when he reached the last flight he would look into the gloom and see a black dog. This made no noise, nor did it move, but Nash would run terrified to the gate on the landing beyond which the nursery lay.

He also said that there were times where he would be playing with his siblings when the black dog would appear, although only he could see it. Sometimes at a party Nash would be aware that the dog was approaching before he saw it. To him, this was a thing of horror and embarrassment. He would have been raised in a Victorian household where natural instincts were often something to be repressed and ignored and the dog served as a reminder of his difficulty in achieving this control.

To the Victorians and other rational thinkers all hallucinations were due to illness or hysteria and held no meaning and this can sometimes the case. The Society for Psychical Research recorded an event where a woman was nursing her sick sister. One day she saw a black retriever sitting on an angle of the stairs and the following day she developed her sister's infection. In this case the woman realised early on that the hallucination was due to the beginning of the invasion of the infection; she did not see a ghost but neither was she mentally unstable.

But it is not true to say that everyone who sees these apparitions is suffering from illness or anxiety and often visions are not meaningless or imaginary. Going back to the Native American example earlier, we could suggest that many people have some form of totemic element in their subconscious but are totally unaware of it until a change in health or another extraordinary circumstance brings it to the fore as a form of symbol. Because they are neither intellectually or culturally prepared for such a happening, this would naturally cause some fright depending on how the symbol or image manifested itself. This is very similar to the folk memory premise already discussed.

In some cases it may be that the lifestyle that the person experiencing the Black Dog in a dream state has can provide some influence on the nature of the dream. The following piece of correspondence comes from the archives of author and research Janet Bord:

"... at the time of my experiences, I was into black magic and Aleister Crowley especially. It may seem unusual, but I had vivid nightmares in which a black dog appeared. I could be having a perfectly normal dream when this animal would just walk into it and turn it all around. It started with a dream about the group Bucks Fizz. I don't like them personally but dreamt I was at a concert of theirs when suddenly, a huge black dog fell from somewhere in the ceiling and tore off the head of the male singer. Also that night I dreamt that a neighbour of mine had been involved in a coach crash where a male singer was left in a coma.

Well, since then if anything bad is about to happen, the black dog walks into my dream and shows me. It is very big with red eyes like embers, and has a coat like hair, through which I can see its muscles. Sometimes it appears with human hands. On one occasion, I dreamt a friend and I were chatting when the dog walked in with hands instead of feet and pushed a dead puppy into her mouth. She miscarried later in actual life."

In considering Black Dog apparitions in dreams and visions we are naturally dealing with a particular time period as of course virtually all of these will occur either during the hours of darkness or the transitory periods of dawn and dusk. This factor of time is of some importance in an examination of the phenomenon. Why should apparitions appear at a particular moment and not another? There is no obvious reason why this should be the case but if it happens then there should be some law which governs the event. If ghosts actually exist then they need to be considered as out of time altogether and so would have to impinge on the natural world of time and space in order to be witnessed. If the events which we are looking at are psychological in some way then there must still be a reason as to why they happen at the time that they do. In either case the cause is at least in part subjective and so the determining factor lies with the witness who is restricted to the clock – a purely physical and man-made object.

In many cases apparitions are not deemed to be random but are connected to either time or to calendar events. There are many cases where ghosts are said to appear on a particular day – New Year's Eve or some festival for example – and so the phenomena would need to be able to make adjustments for variations in the calendar or year. Leap years would be an obvious example. This should lead us to a conclusion that the human subconscious or subjectivity plays a large part in these stories.

As far as Black Dog ghosts are concerned many seem to be witnessed late into the evening, towards the midnight hour. Of the remaining ones, the majority are seen around sunset or at dusk; at those important liminal boundary periods which we have already examined. At these times familiar objects look more unusual, animal eyes can glow eerily and outlines become less distinct. Human vision becomes inhibited and with it the sense between what is physical and what is within the mind is dulled. Moonlight can bring on a dreamy fey mood.

There does not appear to be any pattern to days of the week in Black Dog reports. When considering spirit phenomena more generally, Fridays and Saturdays seem to have some significance but not so much in the case of ghost dogs. There are one or two fleeting references. Morley Adams wrote that the people in Norfolk *"most likely to see the Hell-Hound are those born under the chime hours or towards the small hours of a Friday night."*

Generally, it is said that people born under the chime hours are more receptive to seeing apparitions. The Oxford Dictionary of English Folklore notes that the term chime hours was used particularly in Somerset and East Anglia and alluded to the old monastic hours of night prayer. Even after the Reformation some churches marked these with the ringing of the church bells. A crucial time is said to be midnight. Charles Dickens specified in the first chapter of his novel David Copperfield that it was Friday midnight. In fact the chime hours varied somewhat by location. For instance, at Blaxhall in Suffolk they were 8pm, midnight and 4am. Somerset folklorist Ruth Tongue said that in the West of her county it was believed that anyone born on a Friday between midnight and cock-crow was a chime child and could both see and converse with fairies and ghosts. Moreover, they were understood to have the power of witchcraft and to be able to heal both animals and plants. She believed herself to be one of these people and it was undoubtedly because of this belief that many of the rural folk confided in her about such matters.

Dreams are highly personal and the content, when we can remember it at all, is unique to us as dreamers. But there are rare cases where people report similar dreams at the same time. These are even more unusual when there is a family or other very close connection between the dreamers.

One female witness, commenting on a website article about Black Dogs, describes such an event. In her comment she tells of a dream which she had just had where she was walking by the window of her basement apartment (the writer was from Canada) and she saw a very big and very black dog. She estimates the size as being similar to a pony. The dog was walking slowly and glaring at her. She recalls that in her dream she thought at first that the dog was a hell hound and then decided that perhaps it resembled the devil. She called for her boyfriend to see and he came to the window with his mother. By this point in the dream the dog was at the window growling to get in. The girl and her boyfriend ran to their bedroom but the mother was left behind and was attacked. All the couple could do was listen to her screams.

This was obviously a very frightening dream for the lady involved, but it was made more disturbing by the fact that a short while later she had her mother round for tea and told her about the dream. The mother replied that she had a very similar dream about the same dog on the same night. In her dream the dog attacked a pot bellied pig and the mother got away, but the descriptions of the dog and the night of the dream matched up.

Of course, this is likely to be quite coincidental. Unless the two people involved regularly dreamed similar things we cannot read too much into it, interesting though it is. What does give an interesting insight into the role of dreams is the fact that the daughter, who had used to be a Christian, had been struggling for some time with having left her faith. She took the dream as a confirmation that she had made the wrong choice and subsequently returned to church and renewed her vows. The symbol of the dog, which can be both demonic or protective in this case served both roles. She read the symbol as a devil or demon and this prompted her to return to her faith, where she found that protection. The dream most likely served as a way for her mind to resolve the inner conflict and steer her on the path that she subconsciously wanted to be on.

Recurring dreams are unusual, but some people suffer from them on a variety of subjects. They are more common in children and will usually fade away over time, most likely as the brain develops and begins to process more information and life experiences. But in a few rare cases they can continue for many years, not always with exactly the same thing happening each time but rather with a recurring theme.

One lady, corresponding in 2006, described how she had experienced this phenomena with a Black Dog since the age of 6. In this initial dream she was looking out of her window and saw two dogs fighting each other. One was brown and friendly looking and the other was black and appeared to be more evil. The latter appeared to be attacking the former. The girl (as she was at the time) shouted at the black dog to leave the other one alone and *"pick on someone your own size"*. At this point the black dog looked up at the window and spoke to the girl, saying *"OK I'll get you instead"*. It jumped up at the window, which was half open in the dream, and attempted to get into the room and attack the girl. At this point she woke up terrified.

This dream exhibits a most unusual trait insofar as the dog speaks. As we discovered earlier in the book, this is a very rare attribute in Black Dog folklore and it is also unusual for it to occur in dreams as well. This Black Dog, as a dream symbol, has stayed with the witness and keeps coming into her dreams since this initial happening. As a child of six it is easy to imagine how profound an effect this dream could have had on the psyche and it is plausible to suggest that this may have embedded the image very strongly in the subconscious.

Now, in dreams where the witness is walking outside in any location and the Black Dog appears it will most often just be an observer and not take any form of action or interaction. However, if the witness is inside her own home (in the dream) and sees the dog outside then she will be very scared and close the curtains, although she will still peer through to make sure that the dog is walking in the opposite direction. However, as soon as she does this then the dog will always spot her and try to get through the bedroom window.

In these later dreams the dog still speaks, telling the lady to mind her own business or stop looking at it, always in the same male voice.

It is easy to speculate that the profound nature and effect of the original dream on a young child would lead to the possibility of the same theme continuing in later dreams. In this instance we could argue that the original dream does not necessarily draw on any common folk memory or motif but on something quite ordinary, but the end result certainly feeds into the folklore of the Black Dog. It may be quite natural for the girl to have described the dog in her original dream as evil purely because it was black, larger than the other dog and acting as the aggressor. The evolution of the symbolism in the dreams as they continued causes the dog to begin to match the norms of the folklore in this area though.

Another younger witness – a teenager from Texas – reported that they had seen a cloudy-like, shadow form of a black dog from being a baby until about the age of nine and considered it to be a guardian. In this case the "physical" sightings ceased but then the witness went on to dream about the dog afterwards. Psychologically, if this witness saw the dog as a form of protector, as we discussed in an earlier chapter, then to stop seeing the animal could lead to a sense of loss and worry that they were suddenly unprotected or having to fend for themselves in life. The brain may have compensated for this loss by reintroducing the symbol into the dream state. The witness also claimed that they had a great-great-great grandfather in Ireland who had a guardian grim. Although they do not specify what form this guardian was supposed to have taken, it does add an element of the 'family' type of dog into the account.

THE BLACK DOG IN THE
LANDSCAPE

We have spent some considerable time now considering the nature of the Black Dog, its variants, its purpose and the meaning that it holds as a symbol for those who witness it or have some connection to its folklore. But of course folklore is more than a purely personal experience. The Black Dog exists as a legendary and a traditional phenomenon as well as an individual event. In this chapter we move away from an analysis of the "animal" aspects of the Black Dog and explore its place in our landscape.

We have given some thought to the role of the Black Dog as a guardian as one of its facets in many aspects: of roads, bridges, boundaries, even of treasure troves. When we consider these boundary states as being a connection between our physical world and some 'otherworld' in folklore terms, then we can also consider the Black Dog in these states as having the appearance of coming from the next world. This is certainly true of those stories and sightings where the dog is considered as some form of Hell Hound. There is a real mythological link in these cases, and as such in normal terms of symbolism this would suggest that the dog somehow came from the sky or from the earth. Appearances such as these can be presaged by, or accompanied by, particular meteorological or geological conditions such as storms or (in rarer cases) earthquakes. There are theories put forward which suggest that some ghostly apparitions may be caused by geophysical disturbances.

When analysing these sorts of cases it can be very difficult to establish which aspect is causal and which is the effect. Eyewitness accounts do not often make note of specific sequences of events, for example. Some authors have put forward the suggestion that ghosts seem to favour certain weather conditions, particularly an atmosphere which is particularly heavy, foggy or damp. The argument moves on that this could explain why ghosts often haunt valleys, rivers or ruined castles. These places are all damp.

This theory does not explain a great deal however. We do not see a ghost every time there is a thunderstorm. We have also examined many cases where the weather conditions do not match this theory. There have been similar suggestions in the past that there is a strong link between Black Dogs, particularly the Shuck type, and water courses. In the 1970s researcher Ivan Bunn, as we have seen, went so far as to map and list these sightings and noted the distance in miles between these and the nearest water courses or stretches of water, publishing his results in publications such as Fortean Times and others.

Both these theories probably fall somewhat wide of the mark. With reference to water, although we have examined cases where the Black Dog has a direct link, such as in the cases of bridges, we cannot realise generalise any further. There are relatively few places in the British Isles where one is not far from a stretch of water that could be considered significant, certainly in rural areas but also in more urbanised locations.

In both cases, the links are most likely being used as a way of providing some sort of explanation. In the case of the East Anglian Shuck the proliferation of Scandinavian place names in the areas being studied led to a somewhat tenuous suggestion that the Black Dog could have developed from the mythology of Viking invaders and Odin's "dogs of war" but the idea cannot easily be extrapolated either outwards across the rest of the country or backwards to account for the basis of some early accounts.

With the idea of links to the weather, then mythologies inevitably form around particularly outstanding natural events. The great storm of Widecombe in the Moor on Dartmoor in 1638, where the church was struck by lightning bringing down a pinnacle from the church tower, led to the development of mythology surrounding the Devil having visited the church and his horse having either been tethered to, or hitting, the church as it flew across the sky having claimed a soul from the congregation. Here we see the formation of a morality tale warning people against the dangers of sleeping in church, playing cards or missing church altogether depending on the account. A similar freak storm hit the church at Bungay in the market town of Suffolk and a similar mythology developed around this event, only this time concerning the Black Dog.

The story is probably one of the most famous in the Black Dog canon. Much has been written on the subject and can be easily sourced – fellow folklorist David Waldron has co-authored a book specifically on the subject – and so it is not necessary to go into great detail on it in this work.

In summary, the events surrounding this story take place on August 4th 1577 whilst the people of Bungay were attending a church service. A wild storm shook the building and there was terrible lightning. An undated broadsheet, most likely published in the same year as the storm, was transcribed by Canon Wm. M. Lummis, MC whilst he was vicar of Bungay in 1957. This account tells that "there appeared in most horrid semblance and likeness to the company there assembled, a Dog, as they discerne it, of a black colour." The dog ran down the aisle of the church and "rung the neckes of (two kneeling men) in one instant clene backwards". Another "was griped in ye back and shrivelled up like a piece of leather, or as the mouth of a bag or purse drawen together with a string". He is amazingly said to have survived this encounter. After this the dog ran from the church, but left "sundrie markes of his talons scratched on the stone of the porch".

The dog fled the church for Blythborough, some twelve miles away, where a similar event was said to take place during matins, with the animal killing other members of the congregation and leaving great claw marks in the door of the church. Although there is no remaining evidence of the encounter at Bungay, the door of the church at Blythborough still displays scratch marks said to be those of the claws.

There can be no doubt that at both Widecombe and in Suffolk these storms were real events. The legend and lore has been mapped on in what were far more superstitious times than those that we now live in. It would be quite natural to equate some form of demonic intervention with such a catastrophe in a holy place. The church records that still exist certainly describe the storm, but they do not mention the dog-ghost. The record in the Churchwarden's book records payments made in the aftermath of the storm:

Md. A great terryble &	*Item paid to iiij pore whomen*)	
ferfull tempest at the	*that layed for the Bodyes*)	
hour of procession upon	*of the ij men that were*)	
the Sondaye / suche	*stryckyn dead within the*)	*viij d*
darknes, Rayne, hayle	*steple of the church at ye*)	
Thunder, & lightenyng as	*great tempest that was the*)	
was never sin the lyke	*iiijth of August in ano dmi*)	
	M. ccccc Seventye & Seven)	

In the burial register of the same church is the entry:

1577

The Tem-	*John ffuller & Adam Walker slayne in the*
pest of	*Tempest in the belfry in the tyme of Prayer*
Thunder	*Upon the Lord's Day ye iiijth of August*

This establishing of a canine connection with storms is not unique in folklore. In some parts of America dogs are said to be considered to be conductors of lightning. This is especially the case if the animal is wet and particularly with reference to the dog's tail. Some people are known to have driven their dogs from a property during a thunderstorm in order to protect from a strike. Other animals in folklore who exhibit similar characteristics are horses and mules. Their eyes are said to attract lightning.

In the terms in which we are addressing in this chapter - those of the landscape around us - then we can consider the Black Dog of Bungay to be a sky dog, this being the obvious origination point of a storm.

An obvious connection when looking at sky dogs which should be drawn at this point is to the mythology surrounding the Wild Hunt. Although this book is looking towards considering the psychological and archetypal images surrounding Black Dog folklore and delving too deeply into mythology leads us on a completely different path there is an element of cross-over here. The Wild Hunt is a well-known image which crosses into various cultural mythologies. It sees various forms of a phantasmal leader (sometimes the Devil, sometimes Odin or another God - in the South-West of the United Kingdom even Sir Francis Drake in some cases) leading a pack of otherworldly horses and riders across the night sky, accompanied by baying hounds and other creatures. It is, as you would expect, an omen of death to look upon this monstrous party.

In Teutonic lands the Wild Hunt was often abroad during the Twelve Days of Christmas. This period, when the sun is at its weakest in the Northern hemisphere, represented a time of crisis to primitive man. It was a time when life failed, and elemental chaos rose from the surface of the earth (another landscape boundary we will give more consideration to shortly). For twelve days monsters and ghosts roamed the earth, in some cultures a different animal was dominant each day.

In Guernsey there was a tradition that people travelling at this time were likely to fall foul of will o' the wisps and black dogs. Other countries had their own demons or monsters which were abroad during the period. In an effort to overcome these happenings before the return of the sun fires would be lit, greenery brought into the house and people would guise the spirits to make light of their fears and of the creatures. These things lie behind some of the pagan aspects of Christmas and were quashed by the Church in medieval times. Remnants did remain and appeared in a watered-down form as hobby-horses, hobby-goats or stags and even in one case as a hobby-dog accompanied by a man with a stick. In the next chapter we will examine a more recent version of this latter example.

Sometimes, as the Teutonic Hunt passed through a house on its dreadful route it was said to leave behind on the hearth a little dog, which howled until it woke the whole household:

> "The people then had to get up and brew some beer in egg-shells, whereupon the creature would exclaim: 'Although I am as old as the Bohemian Forest, I never saw such a thing in my life before'. Then it would jump up, rush off and vanish. But if this charm was not applied, the people of the house were obliged to feed the creature well, and let it lie upon the hearth for a whole year, until Wode returned and took it away with him."

Should we consider that this old tradition has some connection with the leaving of a glass of whisky and a carrot by the chimney on Christmas Eve? Are we prepared to take the risk to ignore this tradition, and end up with a fat bearded man and a reindeer bedding down in our fireplace for the next 12 months...?

There is not an exact equivalent legend in Britain but we do find a strange mix of both the Wild Hunt and Black Dog traditions in Wales where it is said that spirits were heard before a funeral took place. These were known either as the Cwn Annwn (dogs of hell), the Cwn bendith eu Mammau (dogs of the fairies) or Cwn Wybir (sky dogs). Their voices were more slight the closer they were to a man, but louder and more like a great hound if they were further away.

Most wild hunts, according to tradition, appear to ride abroad on stormy nights. However there appear to be very few Black Dogs which either forecast storms or cause them. In terms of folklore there is little distinction between these two things. The most well known is obviously the Black Dog of Bungay, already discussed, but it takes quite in-depth research to find many more examples. Marie Lamont, in 1662, said that the devil in the guise of a brown dog helped her to raise a storm. Lamont, who was 18 years old at the time, was tried as a witch in the Scottish parish of Inverkip which was known for its zealous persecution of women as witches in the second half of the seventeenth century. On the subject of dog ghosts of other colours and weather, in Wales white dogs that had a silver eye were said to be able to see the wind.

In Jersey, the Le Tchan du Bouôlé was said to presage a storm. This was said to be a large black dog with the usual saucer eyes which followed people about at night. The name may come from the term Chouans, the Royalist peasants from western France who rose up against the revolutionary government at the end of the eighteenth century. Many of these took refuge in Jersey. It has been suggested that due to the reported size of the dog these men were responsible for the development of the legend by dressing up to fool the local inhabitants.

Moving on from the dogs of the sky we turn our attention to those who are associated more with the physical landscape beneath our feet: the earth. These include those that emerge from the ground or sink into it away from sight in some way. In mythological terms then there is the obvious link with the 'hounds of hell'. Looking at the folklore aspect, which is the concern of this study, then we are looking again at a boundary between the physical world and some 'other' and in this case with a definite physical entrance. Black Dogs that are actually reported to sink into the earth itself are quite scarce, but some use a pond, well or a tree as a gateway.

Beneath the ground itself some passages or caves are said to be occupied by Black Dogs. This is especially the case where a story deals with some lost or buried treasure which is often said to have a guardian such as a Black Dog. We see this replicated still in fiction; from the dog with the typical eyes like saucers in the Hans Christian Anderson story The Magic Tinderbox to Hagrid's use of his pet "dog" Fluffy to guard to hiding place of the Philosopher's Stone in the first Harry Potter novel.

In the United Kingdom treasure-guarding dogs are rare, but in other countries it is more common. In Germany for example the reformer and collaborator of Martin Luther, Philipp Melancthon, recorded that:

> ...*the demon informed a priest where a treasure was hid; the priest, accompanied by one of his friends, went to the spot indicated; they saw there a black dog lying on a chest. The priest, having entered to take out the treasure, was crushed and smothered under the ruins of the cavern."*

The location of this version of the story is debatable. It has been attributed to Nuremburg but there are a number of similar stories with various changes which emanate from the Harz Mountain area.

In the Normandy region of France, the 'Chiens Noirs' appear to be rather more happy to hand over the treasure left by their master's, but only where people have shown kindness to dogs in the first place.

Probably the only parallel story in England comes from the county of Lancashire where we find the talking dog at Dobb Park Lodge, which we referred to at the very beginning of this book.

Dobb Park Lodge was a ruin of a house located in the valley of the Washburn. The exact date of the building is unknown but it has been suggested that its foundations may have been sunk as early as 1311. There is also little recorded about either its occupants or the way that the building was used. An intriguing reference which is crying out to be tied into the following story comes from a Wharfdale historian named Shaw, who wrote that "there was a court held in it after it was dilapidated, called *Dog Court* (my italics), belonging to the Duchy of Lancaster."

The only entrance to the house was by climbing a tower to the rear. At the foot of this tower was a doorway which led down to a dungeon. Local inhabitants were said to have reported hearing strange noises coming from these depths and one of them set out to explore and investigate. He found himself in a series of long winding passages when he heard music coming from ahead of him. Following the sounds he came to a wide, high room as big as a church. A fire was burning in the room, making everything as bright as daylight. In front of the fire stood "a great, black, rough dog, as big as any two or three mastiffs". The dog spoke to the man and said:

> *"Now, my man, as you've come here, you must do one of three things, or you'll never see daylight again. You must either drink all the liquor there is in that glass; open that chest; or draw that sword."*

The chest was large and iron-bound and on top of it stood a glass with a long stem. The sword hung above these two from a peg. The man looked at the three and considered the drink to be the simplest of the tasks he was being offered. He picked up the glass and took one sip (which was as though he was drinking fire). As he did so the lid of the chest flew open and revealed large quantities of gold within. Above, the sword drew itself and flashed like lightening. The man threw down the glass which shattered, spilling the boiling liquid. At the same time the light went out and the music faded, to be replaced by the sound of dogs howling. The man fainted and, when he came to, managed to crawl out of the dungeon by the same route that he had come in.

Among the other subterranean dogs is that guarding the entrance to the passage which was believed to run from the Black Dog Inn at Washford Pyne in Devon (discussed earlier). This pub stands by a crossroads: in folklore this meeting of roads has many associations with witches, burials (of suicides or treasure) and ghosts.

There are many traditions of hidden passages all around the countryside. At Chudleigh, in Devon, a legend tells that a dog was put into a cave and three weeks later it emerged at Bottor Rock in Hennock, some 4 miles away, minus all of its hair. Both of these locations are associates with pixies, which has some significance as dogs are always opposed to fairies.

Welsh fairies have their own dogs which they sometimes leave with humans, reacting later depending on how well the dog has been looked after my its temporary owners. Real dogs are hated by them, however. In Scotland it is said that if dogs chase fairies they return home hairless (and sometimes skinless as well) and appear to have been clawed. For example, two men from Mull were living in a hut in the hills whilst they built a dyke in the Kintail area. One night they heard screaming from the direction of their dwelling but could not see anything. The sound got closer until finally a dark object passed them by. A small dog that they had with them, called 'Dun-Foot' ran off after the noise. When it came back the only hair remaining was on its ears. The coat never grew back properly again, instead resembling a down.

Other aspects of the landscape which can act as crossing points to the underworld may include wells, pools or trees. This latter is the most common of the three with specific connection to dogs. You may find a Black Dog coming out from one, or as we have already seen accompanying a traveller until a tree is reached, at which point it vanishes. In the story of the squire Dennis Rolle (examined in the chapter on Westcountry dogs) the unfortunate man dies under a tree and turns into a Black Dog, which continues his journey.

The tree does not seem to be any more important as a location than any number of alternatives such as a fence or a pool, but we can learn that it can be very important in the adaptation of the Danish folk tale The Tinder Box by Hans Andersen. In this tale a poor soldier meets a witch by a large hollow tree. The witch tells the soldier that if he will descend inside the tree and collect a tinder box for her then she will reward him with money that he really needs.

At the bottom of the hollow tree was a great hall which was lit by three hundred lamps. Around the walls of this hall were three doors, with their keys hanging nearby. Each of these doors led to a room with a chest full of money, but each chest was guarded by a dog.

The first of the chests is full of copper coins and the dog which guards it has eyes as big as tea-cups. The second is full of silver and the dog has eyes as big as mill-wheels; the third contains gold and its guardian has eyes like two round towers.

The soldier proceeds very wisely to collect the copper and silver coins on the witch's apron and exchanges this money for the gold, collects the tinder box and returns from the hall back up through the hollow tree to the surface. He is suspicious of the value of the box and decided to murder the witch by cutting her head off with his sword, before going into town.

Upon striking the tinder box, the soldier discovers that it produces the copper dog. Striking the box twice produces the silver dog and three times yields the gold one. These dogs bring the soldier money and even abduct the princess from the copper castle for short periods of time to visit. Eventually, the dogs save the soldier's life when he is about to be hanged for his presumption, and he marries the princess.

There are very clear motifs in this story which we find more generically, particularly in the descriptions of the dog's eyes. There are also interesting parallels with the story of the dog at Dobb Park Lodge above. The dog that collects the princess for the soldier in Hans Christian Andersen's story has to ascend a copper tower, having already ascended to the earth's surface from the hall beneath the hollow tree. The entrance to Dobb Park Lodge was only upwards, via a tower staircase, and similarly the haunted chamber was down beneath in the dungeon which was accessed from the foot of the stairs. One has to wonder on why these similarities should have come about.

The headless horseman in Washington Irving's tale of the Legend of Sleepy Hollow again enters the earthly plane from a large hollow tree, so this is clearly an important natural bridging point between the worlds. It is probably the case that more research needs to be carried out in the role that trees play in some of these traditions.

We can of course still find remnants of the Black Dog in the landscape around us today. Sometimes the reasoning for this is quite clear and sometimes less so. In cases when the tradition of a black dog haunting is very strong, then the symbol gets adopted as something for which the location is known, in the same way that it is easy to find references to Uncle Tom Cobley at Widecombe on Dartmoor, for example. The story of the Black Dog of Bungay, above, is one of the most famous in the United Kingdom, and hence pubs, shops and even the local marathon are preceded by the term "Black Dog".

Pubs are an instance where we need to not be too hasty to jump to conclusions over derivation of nomenclature however. The fact that a pub is called "The Black Dog" may suggest that there is a local tradition of a haunting but it is no guarantee. The reason for the naming of an old establishment may be lost in time and the original explanation may be as simple as the first landlord having owned a favourite melanistic pet. As is so often the case in folklore and tradition, nothing is a given.

Occasionally, however, we do find references to the Black Dog in modern times that most certainly do relate to the tradition and we will begin the final chapter by examining a couple of these.

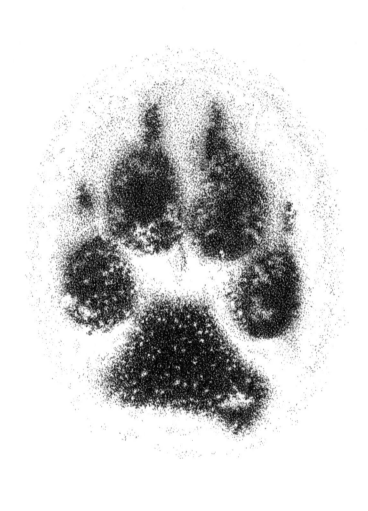

THE BLACK DOG
IN
MODERN TIMES

As we have seen throughout this book there are still a plentiful supply of recent sightings of Black Dogs, as well as many other more modern references in the landscape, in our language and semantics. Despite the many hundreds of years through which Black Dog folklore appears to have existed the motif has not disappeared.

One of the most recent significant instances of global interest in the Black Dog occurred in May of 2014. For this was the month in which physical evidence of its existence was finally proven when the skeleton of the legendary Black Shuck was reported upon in the United Kingdom.

At least, it was if you chose to read the correct news reports.

During an archaeological dig at Leiston Abbey in Suffolk in the previous year, the skeletal remains of a very large dog were found amongst the ruins. The bones, which were said to belong to a male dog, suggested that the animal stood at around seven feet in height, with an estimated weight of 200 pounds.

Initially reported in the local press, the story was of sufficient interest to be picked up by the Daily Mail, a national tabloid newspaper, and from there inevitably onto the internet news sites. At each step the story became more embellished, and more riddled with factual and folkloric inaccuracies, before Yahoo News triumphantly decreed on its website:

> *"Bones of 7ft Hound from Hell Black Shuck 'Discovered in Suffolk Countryside"*

The story is of great interest as a piece of folklore in itself and warrants some deconstruction as a fine demonstration of the way that stories are told, retold and disseminated in the modern age, helping to keep the folklore alive. The local Leiston newspaper presented a fairly short piece which was greatly expanded and illustrated with some fine (over the top and inaccurate) graphical representations of the Shuck by the Mail.

The grave in which the bones were found by an archaeology team from 'Dig Ventures' was approximately twenty inches deep and had no obvious markings attached to it. Pottery fragments found at the same dig level were dated to the 16th century. It was therefore decided that this was the "height of the Shuck's alleged reign" and hence a link to the story could be made.

Of course, it is undoubtedly the case that the skeleton belonged to a large dog, possibly a Newfoundland, which would have been kept at the abbey at the time, as the sensible reportage of the Leiston newspaper happily pointed out. They quoted from an interview with Lisa Westcott Wilkins, the managing director of the archaeology group, who highlighted that the remains were found close to where the abbey kitchen would have been and pointed out that even in medieval times pets were held in high regard.

In point of fact, the only reference to Black Shuck at all in this original article was the headline, which asked in a rather tongue-in-cheek manner "Are these the bones of devil dog, Black Shuck?". The rest of the piece concentrated on the archaeology, as the dig was an unusual example of a project which had been crowdfunded. But there is little appeal in that for a national newspaper, which could however get their teeth into (no pun intended) the suggestion in the leader for the piece.

The Daily Mail therefore ran with the Shuck link and removed the majority of the archaeological elements of the story altogether, apart from the obvious part of the bones having been discovered by archaeologists. Instead they chose to pad their article (which ran to 11 pages once printed from their online version with illustrations) with extensive mentions of the famous Bungay Black Dog case.

By the time the story was re-edited and published on the internet by Yahoo, there was no doubt that the bones of the Shuck had been found. Their article began:

> *"The bones of a seven-foot-long hound from hell have been discovered in the grounds of an ancient abbey in the Suffolk countryside.*
>
> *Black Shuck was believed to have roamed the countryside about 500 years ago. Folk-law (sic) says the giant creature was the hound of hell, with savage claws and burning eyes.*
>
> *According to the Daily Mail, the beast's remains have now been found by archaeologists digging at the site of an ancient abbey, located a few miles from where Black Shuck was said to have killed worshippers in 1577."*

So there you have it. Get your news from the internet and you have definite proof that a legendary creature has been discovered. Look at the 'facts' that are now stated compared to the original article. It is now a hell hound.

This article is a bit of fun in a world which is all too often supplying us with nothing but bad news. It is a useful example of folklore in action and it serves a valuable purpose in helping to keep the traditions alive, in the same way that paranormal television programmes made "for entertainment purposes only" help to foster a continuing interest in areas which help to keep rich traditions going in the modern world.

The Black Shuck discovery continues to draw on a motif which has been with us for a long time, and which still affects a number of people in the twentieth and twenty-first centuries, even if they are unaware of the legends. Sometimes they can be completely unaware because of their age. For example, Nikki Hatch sent me this story from her childhood:

"I grew up in Liphook. Just under the iron bridge and turn left. Wheatsheaf Enclosure – the road leading to the golf course and further on to the coachroad. My mother was in the habit of walking the dogs in the early evening around dusk. It was one such evening and I was in a pushchair so I guess I would have been about 2 or 3 years old (1965/6). The poodles apparently stopped at the crossroads (where the main road intercepts (sic) the coachroad), staring towards the right turn and growled. I remember seeing a large black dog. It's (sic) mouth was very red. It's (sic) coat was rough and coarse. It just stood looking down at me. I apparently said to my mother 'Mummy, I don't like that black dog'. She could see nothing. I remember it felt threatening although, to my recollection it did nothing.

My mother tells me that she saw a black dog herself only a short distance along the same path. It was standing on the path looking towards her. She bent to pick up the poodles and it was gone although she couldn't see where it could have jumped without her noticing."

Nikki says that it was many years before she realised that black dog sightings were so common. At the age that she estimates she was when this sighting happened there was obviously no way that she could have known about, or consciously drawn upon any folk motif surrounding the Black Dog. So what did she see? Was it a real dog, and if so why did her mother not see it as well? Too many years have passed for us to ever know for certain.

There is an interesting afterword to this, to bring it into the 21st century. Researching the location a little more prior to publishing this story did not turn up any reported sightings of other 'ghostly' black dogs for certain. But it did provide a link to the Liphook community website, which yielded a page concerning dogs in the same general area. A person posting on the 'Local Talkback' page (a forum for local residents to air their views) discussed an incident where two black Labradors were running loose in the road, causing cars to slow down. The writer and a colleague had endeavoured, and failed, to catch the dogs which ran off across a field. Two further people commented on the post, one to say that they had been involved in a serious car accident taking evasive action to avoid loose dogs there, and another to say that they had often seen a single black dog on that stretch of road.

Whilst we should not entertain the possibility too strongly that there is any sort of 'otherworldliness' about the dogs being commented upon on this website, the link to Nikki's story – in the same manner as the Black Shuck's bones – is the stuff of which folklore can be made in the right (or wrong) hands.

In a final postscript to her correspondence, Nikki pointed out that there is a pub at the end of the coachroad in the area, on the A3 road, called The Black Fox. She wondered if this had any significance to her experience. There is unlikely to be any connection at all to this, but of course as we have already discussed to some degree, pub names are another example of the Black Dog perpetuating into modern times.

According to a survey of English pub names conducted in 2011, there are 18 public houses in the United Kingdom called "The Black Dog" and slightly more than the same amount again called the Dog Inn. Many of these will have no folklore connection at all and may be named after a family pet, racing dog or hunting hound. Others draw more heavily on old stories and traditions.

We have already examined the case of the Black Dog of Uplyme and the guest house at the location of this Dog (originally opened as a pub) was most definitely named after this tradition. Others claim an historic or folkloric link which is a little more tenuous.

In the village of Yapton in West Sussex, for example, stands a building with boarded up windows and most of the letters missing from a sign which used to tell passers-by that this was called "The Olive Branch". This pub, which closed down in 2014, was previously called the "Black Dog". The claim made for the name was that it came from the tale of a smuggler who was drinking at the pub when he was discovered by revenue men and was killed. It was said that the man's loyal pet, a black dog, ran thereafter around the village looking for his lost master. Even in death, the dog's ghost is said to still be searching.

Whilst there are quite strong traditions in some places of ghost dogs searching in this way, there is little either tradition or history to back up the story in this case. It may well be the case, therefore, that the story developed later in a similar way to those many pubs which are the "most haunted pub in the country".

There are other Black Dog traditions to be found in the Yapton area and these may have had some influence on the naming as well in this case. It was said at one time that villagers there would leave their house doors open so that the Black Dog was able to roam freely because otherwise it would become angered and howl.

If the stories and legends are strong enough, then the name naturally becomes integrated not just into the name of the local pub, but other buildings, businesses or organisations will also take it up. Visit any one of the number of locations which are connected to Arthurian legend and you will see this in action. King Arthur has car parks, tearooms, shops and guest houses. He is quite a property magnate. The same often happens with the Black Dog.

However, as we have already noted, some caution needs to be exercised in tying in too closely the folklore of the Black Dog with instances of its name being referred to. This refers to place names, but also to some more obscure references in older and more recent history.

Looking at other place names we find the hamlet of Blackdog, situated two miles to the north of the border of Aberdeen. Neither this, nor the Blackdog Inn would appear to have any immediate connections to the folkloristic angle of the name.

The Devon village of Black Dog would again appear to have tenuous links. Although there are (ghostly) Black Dog sightings in the area, this does not appear to be the root of the name as older maps of the area mark the village as Black Boy, which would suggest a more likely link to the slave trade. The local inn was also named The Black Boy, before changing its name to the Blue Boy and finally to the Black Dog, although this was most likely a reference to a previous publican's hunting dog rather than to the legend. Many people still tie the name of the village to the legends of the Black Dog and it is very easy to make assumptions which often stick in this way, changing and developing the folklore of an area. But then, this is what folklore is all about at the end of the day; tracing original roots can be a real challenge.

A now defunct prison in Dublin, which was named The Black Dog, was again named from a local hostelry in the area of Browne's Castle where the building was located. In this case though, some slightly tenuous folkloric link developed later in the form of the legend of a prisoner incarcerated there who was sentenced to death for rape and murder. The man committed suicide in the prison and it was later said that his spirit haunted the jail. He was said to be responsible for a number of deaths in the local area, whilst in the guise of "a wild beast". Whilst a dog is not specifically named in this case, it is easy to see how the folklore of the Black Dog could have contributed to this story as there are obvious links to the evil side of both the jail and the man's character. Parallels may be drawn with the earlier case of Newgate jail.

The darker aspect of the motif of the Black Dog can also be found in literature. As well as the obvious links (such as the Hound of the Baskervilles) and other fiction titles which have been published specifically about the legendary Black Dog, the name has been used in other titles as a signifier of mood. For example, the 1992 novel Black Dogs by Ian McEwan is about Europe in the times after the Nazis post World War II. The title draws on the themes of darkness, evil and depressed states which are often conjured up by the Barguest and similar types of Black Dogs in folklore. It is quite widely known that the British Prime Minister during this time, Winston Churchill suffered from bouts of depression which he called his "Black Dogs". McEwan based the name on this fact. We still find this aspect referred to in other ways, as for example there is a Black Dog Institute which studies, diagnoses and treats forms of depression such as bipolar disorders.

Further back in history we can also find items which reference the more negative connotations of the dog which we have discussed previously in this book. For example, The Black Dog was the name of a pewter or copper coin which was found in the Caribbean during the reign of Queen Anne. In this case the negative aspect comes from the fact that the coinage was made from debased silver.

Novelist Stephen Booth also published a crime title, Black Dog, in 2000 which is set in the Peak District. Again this does not specifically relate to folklore.

The name comes up in other forms of entertainment too. A British group specialising in house and other forms of electronic music formed in 1989 with the name of The Black Dog. And well known British group Led Zeppelin famously recorded a song called Black Dog, which was the opening track on their fourth album. In this case the song was written in reference to an un-named black Labrador Retriever which was hanging around Headley Grange studios where the group recorded. The song lyrics refer to the sexual advances of the singer and were said to be based on the fact that the dog, although somewhat aged, also displayed similar traits. One lyric in the middle of the song however, "eyes that shine burning red, dreams of you all through my head" do appear to reference the Black Dog legends.

There is a well known brand of Scotch Whisky called "Black Dog". In this case the name comes from the term for a particular type of fly used in salmon fishing. The moral of the story is that one can never assume that the term Black Dog will specifically refer to the folklore, myths or legends that you would expect.

One modern aspect where you can be more certain of links to older folklore is in calendar customs, festivals and traditions. There are many of these, often using green men, Morris dancers and the like, but the most well known are probably 'obby 'oss traditions such as those found in Padstow or Minehead. The actual origins of these festivals are often shrouded due to their age but are often linked to fertility rites and other pagan celebrations. They are a wonderful preservation of old traditions.

Considering the prolific nature of Black Dog folklore it is rather surprising that this does not seem to make an appearance in these traditions. There was one notable exception. In 1993 members of the Devon based Pennymoor Singaround folk group, including husband and wife team Ken and Clare Penney, Len Christopher and Pat Barker decided to create their own 'Obby 'Oss festival, which became known as "The Running of the Black Dog".

In this case the new tradition was based not on old customs of fertility or anything else, but drew on the folklore of the Black Dog, more specifically the Black Dog of Torrington discussed earlier, to create an event which just allowed people to enjoy themselves and some traditional English custom and song.

The Black Dog they created measured ten feet long from nose to tail and about four feet wide. It was led on a processionary route which took in much of the area around Morchard Bishop (where the Torrington Black Dog was often sighted) and was danced by a succession of carriers, led by a "ticer", similar to the traditional fool character and accompanied by a band of musicians and walkers. A traditional tune, renamed "The Black Dog Polka" was used to accompany the 'oss.

Prior to the departure of the 'oss and party from the London Inn pub in Morchard Bishop, a "proclamation" would be made as follows:

> *"My Lords, Ladies and Gentlemen, since time immemorial, gentlefolk from all parts of The County of Devon, have reported their encounters with the Great Black Dog of myth, song and legend. But never more so than on the road that runs between Morchard Bishop and the village of Black Dog.*
>
> *In these parts, the sighting of the Black Dog has always been taken as an omen of good fortune, for it is believed that the Dog is the guardian of great treasure.*
>
> *Tonight, as at every year at this time, we invite you to join us as we dance our own great Dog on the road to the Black Dog Inn, and join in with the music and dance that herald's the Dog's progress through the lanes."*

The spirited nature that this statement would have instilled in those listening allows us to forgive some of the small factual inaccuracies which it contains!

The new tradition has sadly now ceased to be carried on and so the Black Dog must return back to the more obscure annals of folklore once again in this sense which is a great shame. The 'oss still exists in a barn somewhere and we must hope that this is at least preserved and not lost to the ravages of time.

As this book has hopefully demonstrated the aspects of Black Dog folklore still amongst us are many and varied. After hundreds of years of both tradition and actual eyewitness accounts, there is still far less knowledge about the motif than would maybe be expected. This is shown from the fact that to this day sightings are still recorded or submitted and often with no obvious prior knowledge of the phenomena. This statement brings us full circle from the introduction to this volume, which began with a modern sighting sent from an eyewitness overseas who had taken some time to be able to tell her story as she thought she was alone in her experience and did not know how to discuss it.

This study, coupled with the extensive gazetteer in the appendix which follows, will hopefully go some way to enable more people to understand their own experiences if they have them, or to increase knowledge and discussion of a prolific and yet under-represented subsection of folklore more generally.

It will perhaps be pleasing to conclude, as the Running of the Black Dog concluded, with their own sung "Farewell to the Black Dog":

We stand here together in Devon's fair land,
Goodbye fare thee well, we wish you all well.
Before we must part let us join hand in hand,
Goodbye fare thee well, we're homeward bound.

The Dog he has led us this night through the lanes,
Goodbye fare thee well, we wish you all well.
But now he must leave us before the moon wanes,
Goodbye fare thee well, we're homeward bound.

Farewell to the Dog and the Ticer as well,
Goodbye fare thee well, we wish you all well.
Wherever he bides no mortal may tell,
Goodbye fare thee well, we're homeward bound.

Farewell to the players and all gathered here,
Goodbye fare thee well, we wish you all well.

Black Dog Folklore

The Dog will await you again next year,
Goodbye fare thee well, we're homeward bound.

Farewell to the Summer and to the Green Man,
Goodbye fare thee well, we wish you all well.
May he bring back Spring time as soon as he can,
Goodbye fare thee well, we're homeward bound.

Let's into the Ale House and call for our grog,
Goodbye fare thee well, we wish you all well.
We'll all raise a glass to the health of the Dog,
Goodbye fare thee well, we're homeward bound.

Appendix

A GAZETTEER OF UK BLACK DOG SIGHTINGS AND TRADITIONS

The collection of reports in any area of folklore research is, of course, an ongoing task, There is no finite end point, no time where suddenly old traditions stop coming to light, or eyewitness accounts stop coming in. This compendium of legends, traditions and eyewitness reports of Black Dog apparitions should therefore be considered a snapshot.

The archive of reports which I hold is quite substantial and to put it into this book in its entirety would be unmanageable – it would lead to probably a multi-volume work. Therefore, for brevity, I have distilled the information of each archive entry into a couple of lines of text. Some records where the location is unknown have been included if the content of the report is of sufficient interest; many have been omitted if they are too vague in both content and location data.

Each entry, as far as possible, tries to give detail as to whether the report is an eyewitness sighting or a tradition along as much location and time detail to make the data useful.

This archive is not, at the time of writing, available in the public domain in its full detail but I am happy to discuss the detail of any entries in more detail with interested parties if the information is of use to them. Similarly, I am of course happy to receive further sightings or account from people who may have them. Email contact may be made via the publishers of this book, or The Folklore Society.

Entries are listed alphabetically by county, and then by location within that county. In most cases traditional older county names have been used in keeping with the older research archives where they may also appear, and to make sense of the time and place data.

Appendix

Catalogue of Black Dog Sightings
and Traditions in the UK

ABERDEENSHIRE

1. Black Dog Rock: Name of location four miles north of the estuary of the Don, below the high tide mark
2. Black Doggie: Name of a game played in Aberdeenshire by children. A version of "Drop Handkerchief".

ANGLESEY

3. Aberglaslyn: Man returning home from Porthmadoc has a huge mastiff the size of a calf walk up to him from somewhere, before vanishing
4. Amlwch: Three holidaymakers walking down a lane hear growling and turn to see black dog with red eyes. No date, but reported in 2008
5. Llanfachraeth: Early 20th century – phantom dog seen close to Dronwy farm on multiple occasions. Reported to vanish into thin air
6. Llanfechell: 1910-1915 – man cycling in a lane at dusk sees a black dog a few yards ahead. It kept pace before vanishing at a junction
7. Llangoed: 1975-1978 – multiple witnesses see a ghostly apparition of a white dog running along a lane before suddenly disappearing
8. Rhosgoch: A farm labourer sees a dog which two other men cannot see. They tease him about it before the dog appears to them in a barn
9. Rhosneigr: A man returning from work on a pushbike reaches a bridge at Afon Crugyll and sees two black dogs emerge from the water. They run alongside the bike until he reaches home, by which time they have vanished

ARGYLLSHIRE

10. Colonsay: Folk tale of McPhie's Black Dog, which has multiple variants

11. Craignish: Phantom dogs were said to be regular visitors at Caisteal a Choin Dubh (Castle of the Black Dog)

12. Isle of Mull: Black Dog of Ardura – seen in 1909 by a doctor who let it into Lochbuie House thinking is was a real dog. The owner of the house died soon after

13: Isle of Mull: Black Dog of Ardura – seen in 1914 in the headlights of his car by a doctor visiting a patient in Lochbuie. The patient died that night

14: Isle of Mull: Black Dog of Ardura – seen on 13th November 1915 by Miss White and recorded the next day on Lochbuie notepaper by 'L. Chamanyon'

15. Knapdale: Regular phantom black dogs at Dun a Choin Dubh (Fort of the Black Dog). See also Craignish above

16. Unknown location: 2½ year old girl sees a black dog with differing coloured eyes in the garden. Her mother used to see them in Essex when she was aged between 5 and 8

AYRSHIRE

17. Kilmarnock: A large black dog runs round and round a horse, forcing it to stop and saving the horse and rider from a disaster. No further information

18. Unknown location: Folk poem or song about a black dog collected in 1827

BANFFSHIRE

19. Bus' (Bush) Road: Large black dog often seen on the road linking the village of Knockandhu with the Braes of Glenlivet

Appendix

BEDFORDSHIRE

20. Dunstable: A tradition of ghostly black dogs the size of retrievers in the fields at night and that to shout at them will court death

21. Harlington: Black dog seen on a lane to the east of the village on multiple occasions in the 19th century

22. Kensworth: Shuck type dog with one eye said to haunt the Bury Hill footpath and claimed to have been seen by many people in the 19th century. Still believed in in the late 20th century

23. Luton: A man reports seeing a black dog in 1981

BERKSHIRE

24. Hoe Benham: Multiple reports from the early 1900s of a black dog that turns into a donkey which stands on its hind legs

BRECKONSHIRE

25. Brecon: A black terrier appears at the house of a man who falls ill. He dies and the dog hides under his bed. At the funeral it appears at the vault and disappears an hour after the burial. It has red eyes and is believed to be the devil's dog.

26. Brecon: A woman who is unkind to animals is said to be accompanied by a large black mastiff with glaring eyes and red eyelids

27. Clyro: The Llowes road was said to be haunted by a black dog, as well as phantom horses

28. Llanwrtyd: Parish church contains a short stair passage which used to be known as Twll y Ci Du (The Hole of the Black Dog)

BUCKINGHAMSHIRE

29. Aylesbury: A farm labourer at a nearby village, going

to milk cows in a field crosses another field to a gap in the hedge and finds a large black dog in the gap every night. Finally he hits it with his yoke and it vanishes

30. Bedfordshire border: A protective black dog was said to be found on the border between Bedfordshire and Buckinghamshire. It accompanied people who had fears of travelling there

31. Savernake Forest: A black dog crossed the A4 in front of two people at 1.30am. No further details

32. Stewkley: Late 1800s, a large black dog would often run after dark beside a dog cart between Stewkley and Soulbury where it disappeared.

33. Tingewick: A dog with no head is seen in the garden of retired police inspector Arthur Springer in 1916. The apparition was allegedly captured on film as the family posed for a photo

CAMBRIDGESHIRE

34. Abbey House: Various people in the early 1900s hear the whining and howling of 'Old Jacob's Dog' in the grounds of the house. It was said to be the dog of Jacob Butler who died in 1765

35. Arbury: Summer of 1970 – a couple driving at night near the junction of Arbury Road and Kings Hedges Road see a dog jump over their car bonnet and disappear through an allotment

36. Barnack: There is a tradition of a dog in this area but no further details

37. Bull Dog Bridge: Story of the ghost of a dog who saved a servant girl who was attacked by a passing friar. The dog savaged the man but was stabbed by his knife before he died. The bridge was renamed White House Bridge

38. Croxton Road: Black dog said to walk a path from the old Caxton gibbet to the crossroads. Referred to as Auld Shuck

39. Devil's Dyke: Traditional account – a dog is said to

roam the area around the dyke

40. Little Downham: Woman reports in 1950 that her grandmother saw a dog at Little Downham

41. Littleport: Shuck type dog used to patrol the road between Littleport and Brandon Creek. It was said to have been hit by a car in 1906 and was never seen again

42. Market Deeping: There is a traditional account from this area but no further details

43. Old Fletton: 1930s – a man met a Shuck type dog twice. Both times the dog vanished into a pond by the side of the road

44. Slough Lane: Said to be haunted by 'The Shug Monkey', a creature that appeared to be a cross between a dog with a rough coat and a monkey with large shining eyes. The animal could move on either two legs or four. Seen in 1897 by Martha Higgs

45. Spinney: Sighting reported in 1954 telling of a woman who once saw a dog glaring at her

46. Stanground: A traditional account exists from this area, but no details are known

47. Unknown location: A woman in Cambridge reported in 2004 that she had seen a dog with a hard looking face the night before her father died

48. Upware: A report from the 1940s on the marshes near to 'Spinney Abbey'

49. Welney: There is a traditional account from the marshes between Welney Road and the river

50. Whittlesey: A report of a dog seen here but no further information

51. Woodcraft Castle: A traditional account from this location but no details known

CARMARTHENSHIRE

52. Cwrt y Cadno: A man from Cilewm has to return to Cwrt y Cadno late at night and is asked by a wizard if he is afraid of the journey over the mountain, which he says he is.

On the way back the man is accompanied by a dog he takes to be a spirit sent by the wizard

53. Kidwelly: A man returning to Kidwelly across the fields is accompanied by a black dog acting as a guardian. A similar variant is also associated with other local places

54. Laugharne: A woman going into town late on business sees a large dog on the way back which sits down and screams so loudly that she faints. She believes it to be a punishment for disobeying her mother who told her not to go

55. Trelech: An old tradition of dogs heard before burials, known as Cwn Annwn (Dogs of Hell), Cwn benditheu Mammau (Dogs of the Fairies) or Cwn wybir (Sky Dogs). They were said to get louder the farther away they were and quieter when closer

CHESHIRE

56. Barthomley: Report of a dog which ran from the Rectory to some farm building. There is also a ghost of a White Lady in the nearby Church Fields

57. Bunbury School: A white dog with chains is seen in the lane

58. Godley Green: A yellow dog is seen in the 1890s on separate occasions by a fishmonger, a child and a woman. The dog is said to be attached to a house now demolished

59. Spurstow Hall: A dog is said to run past the gates of the building

60. Witlington: A black dog accompanies a woman missionary through some woods when she sees a man of bad character approaching her with possible evil intent

CORNWALL

61. Callington: A dog ghost "as big as a yearling, with eyes as tea-cups as flaming" walks a route from Mark Valley Mine to Stoke Climsland

62. Crosscombe Manor: An old tudor house at Trevellas

near St Agnes. A black dog enters the house, runs upstairs and vanishes

63. Darley Ford: A ghost seen as either a black dog, or a man carrying a bundle of sticks, walks a route from Darley Ford to Battens. It is thought to be that of Vincent Darley (d.1764). Sightings recorded at Botternell Turning, Berriow Bridge, near Berriow and Battens.

64. Dinham Manor: A tudor manor by the River Camel. A black dog is reported to run up the drive, sometimes accompanied by an old woman

65. Gulwal: Near Penzance. In the 19th century a widow is walking in a field and sees a strange, spotted dog. She sees it again on another occasion but her friend with her cannot. She spoke to it and it turned into her late husband

66. Harlyn: A black dog haunts the old house which was the seat of the Peters family

67. Helston: In the early 1900s a Wesleyan minister is often confronted on the road by a black dog. He lashes out at it with his cudgel but it passes straight through the animal

68. Land's End: At the turn of the 20th century a man travelling to stay at the 'First and Last Inn' encounters a pack of hounds. Nobody in the area owns dogs of this nature and the locals believe he has seen the Wisht Hounds

69. Launceston: A dog ghost known as the 'Bloodhound of Launceston' is said to haunt the town

70. Launceston: A resident of Launceston reports in 1967 that their mother's cousin would not down a little lane at St Stephens because it was said to be haunted by a black dog

71. Lewannick: A report in 1930 says that a Lewannick man is thrown onto a stoneheap when he tried to bar the way of a dog

72. Liskeard: Ghost associated with a man who was a carrier, compelled to travel a route from Liskeard to Launceston "as many Saturdays after death as before". Seen near Berriow Bridge (see Callington entry above)

73. North Hill: A dog passes between three people out walking in the 1850s

74: North Hill: A report in 1930 of a man who sees a dog on the way to a bridge. The dog vanishes when he threatens it with a stick

75. Porthcurno Cove: Account of a spectral ship associated with a strange man who lived at Chygwiden. He was said to hunt in all weathers with his servant, or the devil and his hounds. When the man died and was buried, dogs gathered at the graveside and disappeared when the earth was thrown in

76. St Austell: Account from 1780 of a party of boys hearing a horse approaching and seeing a large dog with shaggy coat and fiery eyes passing through a closed gate

77. Tintagel: A black dog is said to be seen in a lane running down to Tintage

78. Wheal Vor Mine: Haunted by "troops of little black dogs" as the result of a disaster. Catastrophes at the mine were said to be presaged by the appearance of a white rabbit or hare

79. Whitborough: An evil spirit in the shape of a black dog was said to have appeared at Midsummer Eve festivities at Kennick Farm, leading to the event being discontinued for fear that giants buried in the tumulus were annoyed

CUMBERLAND

80. Armnoth House: A ghostly figure of a large dog was said to be seen every year swimming across the lake where a bride was drowned before her wedding feast

81. Penrith: A knight hunting in a forest near Carlisle is caught in a storm and sees "a great hound with fiery jaws". He calls out in his fear for St Simeon, who appears carrying a hunting horn

82. Shap: 1937 – drivers on the A6 report a dog which runs in front of their cars and over a stone wall with a sheer drop on the other side

DENBIGH

83. Cynwyd: A man returning from a fair is followed by a black dog with red eyes. It vanishes by the time he has reached his farm gate

84. Henilan: A man driving slows at a road junction and sees a large black dog with glowing eyes in his headlights

85. Ruthin: A report published in 1930 says that the writer's grandparents were riding on horseback one evening. The grandmother sees a large mastiff and at the same time her horse shies. The grandfather sees nothing and his horse is unaffected

DERBYSHIRE

86. Calver: A report in 1973 states that a woman is accompanied along the road by a dog which walks through a wall

87. Holmesfield: An 1895 says that two people are out walking. One of them sees a dog but the other cannot see it. The event seems to foretell a death

88. Stoney Middleton: A Methodist minister was once said to have been accompanied by a dog when he was approaching dangerous looking men

89. Tunstead Milton: A woman sees a dog walk behind her before vanishing

90. Tunstead Milton: A woman is said to have been protected by a dog when walking in the area

91. Upper Booth: 1930 – a woman sees a dog which passes through a fence

DEVON

92. A30 – a black dog appears in front of a car being driven between Exeter and Okehampton in 1969 causing the driver to brake and swerve. The incident prompts a string of correspondence in the local press

93. Abbot's Way: Dartmoor – this is said to be a favourite hunting ground of the Whisht Hounds

94. Blackmoor Gate: 1939 – a black dog with three sheep runs into the middle of the road and it hit by a bus on Christmas Eve. Neither the driver or the passengers can find any trace of it

95. Bradford: In the first quarter of the 20th century a large black dog was seen at midnight

96. Bradworthy: A large headless dog was seen by several people around the beginning of the 20th century. It moved quickly and with no noise and was supposed to be seen before ill-fortune

97. Branscombe: It has been said that there are two ghost dogs on the cliff near Littlecombe Shoot. One is brindled and the other is black. Both are said to have horns

98. Bratton Fleming: The rector here between 1818 and 1838 was said to keep magical books. He had a black dog which he took to church with him

99. Bridestow: A woman was said to have seen the Whisht Hounds in Burleigh Woods, probably around 1939

100. Buckfastleigh: Graveyard has the tomb of Richard Cabell of Brooke. He was said to have had the Whisht Hounds chase him across Dartmoor at his death

101. Buckfastleigh: 1972 – Cecil Williamson says that he meets a dog in the churchyard and that when he goes to touch it his hand passes through

102. Chittlehampton: A dog runs along Hudscot Plain at midnight

103. Chittlehampton: Denys Rolle dies beneath a tree in 1797 and a black dog is said to continue the walk. This may be the same animal as the previous entry

104. Chudleigh Arch: A shadowy figure like a dog is said to haunt the Exeter to Newton Abbot Road, turning under an arch to Chudleigh via Ugbrook Park

105. Crosscombe: Martinhoe – Sir Robert Chichester is said to roam the countryside in penance for his wicked deeds. He sometimes appears as a black dog, or sometimes

in a flaming car drawn by four elephants

106. Daddy Hole Plain: Torquay – a legend of two hounds representing the Devil's pack

107. Dartmoor: 1972 – a man sees a dog in his house. When he tries to strike it with a poker it explodes and damages the roof and the windows

108. Dean Combe: Buckfastleigh – A weaver continues to appear after his death and is banished by the local vicar. He is transformed into a black dog and bound to emptying a pool with a perforated nut-shell

109. Dewerstone: A headless black dog is said to haunt the valley

110. Dewerstone: Said to be the meeting place of the Whisht Hounds

111. Diptford: Towards the end of the 19th century a farmer's wife runs away with her lover. They set off in a horse and trap and a black dog rushes out as they pass the quarry. The horse shies and the woman falls into the quarry and breaks her neck

112. Doccombe: A shadowy form like a black dog is said to haunt the main road, near Moretonhampstead. It chases people as far as Cossick Cross and jumps over the road at the edge of an oak scrub

113. Down St Mary: Part of the route for the Torrington Black Dog. It was said that you could hear the wall being knocked down by the school as it passed but there was never any physical damage

114. Dulverton to Molland Road: 1984, about 8.30pm – a witness reports seeing "an enormous black animal like a large Great Dane" in the headlights of his car

115. Fitzford: Tavistock – the ghost of Lady Howard is traditionally said to be seen on the road from Tavistock to Okehampton, either in the form of a black dog or riding a coach preceded by a black dog with one eye in the middle of its forehead

116. Frithelstock: 1932 – a dog is seen on a new road cut around the hillside where the Priory used to stand

117. Gidleigh Castle – known for having a black dog with red staring eyes

118. Gidleigh Park Hotel: During the Second World War a man who lived at the farm at the side of the hotel saw a large white dog coming towards him, which vanished

119. Great Torrington: A woman from Great Torrington is out riding and sees a dog which causes her pony to shy. Connected to the Black Dog of Torrington run

120. Hayne: There are stories of a large black dog haunting the park

121. Holne: Bench Tor – a woman saw the Whisht Hounds coming over the brow of the tor, circa 1949

122. Hound Tor: Report written in 1965 of a woman riding at Hound Tor who sees a huge black dog come out of the rocks. It follows her home and disappears as she is looking at it

123. Ilsington: A black dog haunts the road to Lenda farm and walks on its hind legs. It was said to have been seen by the uncle of a local farmer driving a pony and trap

124. Kingston: 1870 – a girl of ten is walking down Kingston village street one evening at dusk and sees a black dog with eyes like "coals of fire". It came up and sniffed her before trotting off. The dog was seen at other times by other villagers

125. Lydford: The driver of a coach crossing the moor at twilight sees a black dog on the moor

126. Lydford: 1982 – a man sees a pig-snouted dog with no eyes in a field

127. Mamhead: A large dog used to sit on the wall at Westleigh Farm, on Obelisk Hill

128. Meldon: An old man tells in 1895 that as a boy he heard the Whisht Hounds coming down past Yes Tor towards Meldon when returning from a hunt and that all of the horses were bathed in sweat and needed grooming afterwards

129. Newton Poppleford: The ghost of a mongrel haunted the Southern Cross Guest House. The owner says that she

saw it a couple of hundred times

130. Newton St Cyres: A girl was murdered by her uncle in a cottage and an indelible bloodstain was left. It was said that if the outside door was open a black dog would walk past on its hind legs at a certain time

131. North Bovey: A ghost in the form of a great black dog is said to howl on a certain night at the head of Week Plantation

132. Okehampton: A woman with a donkey sees a black dog in the lane by the castle grounds. The donkey refused to walk any further. At the same spot a man walking his dog cannot go any further as the dog refuses to move

133. Okehampton: Historic account of the coachman at Okehampton and his passengers being accompanied by a black dog

134. Okehampton: A woman walking in a wood is accompanied by a black dog which seems to protect her

135. Pinkery Pond: A report that a black dog haunts Pinkery Pond seeking revenge for modern farming methods by killing sheep. This is probably an amalgamation of the Beast of Exmoor sightings and the legend of the ghost of a farmer which is said to haunt the area for the same reason

136. Plymouth: Sir Francis Drake is said to be one of the people who leads the Wild Hunt in this area

137. Postbridge: A local tradition of a black dog "as big as a donkey" which patrols the village at night and once jumped over a wall in front of a man

138. Postbridge: A ghostly bloodhound was said to run out from Moretonhampstead each night and snuffle in the ditch opposite a tomb looking for beer thrown out by a teetotal convert

139. Postbridge: Ephraim's Pinch – a white dog, similar to an Afgan Hound was seen during the war in the area of this hill

140. Princetown: A boy of about six sees a pack of black hounds when visiting an old country house, but his sister and parents cannot see them

141. Roborough: A man walking from Princetown to Plymouth sees and hears a black dog, the size of a Newfoundland. His hand passes through when he tries to pat it. It accompanies him to a crossroads when it disappears in an explosion

142. South Brent: Hearsay tells of a dog on South Brent road, but the exact site in uncertain

143. Spreyton: 1682 – the second wife of Philip Furze is said to infest the house as a poltergeist, sometimes appearing as a black dog

144. St Giles in the Wood: In the 1870s, a girl is out walking with her father and is accompanied by a dog, which vanishes

145. Talaton: A dog is said to haunt the road at Talaton and Clyst Honiton

146. Teignmouth: The husband of a couple who own a country inn dies. Shortly after his death the widow and her daughter hear a dog outside but when they speak to it, it leaves. The widow believes that it is her husband's spirit

147. Thorverton: A legend of a black dog, but no further details

148. Tiverton: A black dog is reported as being seen here, but no further details

149. Torrington: A black dog is plotted as travelling between Morchard Bishop and Winkleigh

150. Torquay: A house in the Warberries was said by tradition to be haunted by a black, curly-haired dog

151. Uplyme: A black dog is said to patrol Haye Lane and cross the border at midnight. In 1856 a woman saw a black dog with fiery eyes which swelled and dispersed as a cloud. Her husband saw only sea mist

152. Uplyme: Legend that a black dog used to a farmer company in a local farmhouse. One day he tried to chase it out and it ran upstairs and escaped through the chimney. When the farmer hit the spot where is vanished a box of money fell out

153. Uplyme: 1959 – a family report seeing a dog

float across the road

154. Vitifer: A miner used to be accompanied across the moor by a black dog when going to and from his home

155. Warren House Inn: 1930s – a man passing the pub at about 12.30am on a pony sees a black curly dog running alongside him. It followed for about 300 yards and then vanished

156. Washfield: Circa 1887 – A dog is seen on the road at the back of Worth House by a boy of seventeen. He kicks at it and it vanishes. It is seen by another man soon afterwards

157. Washford Pyne: Legend of a tunnel from Berry Castle earthworks to the crossroads. The entrance was said to be guarded by a black dog at the time of the Civil Wars

158. Welcome: A white dog haunts the cliff at Sandown Cross between Welcome and Hartland

159. West Worlington: Around the end of the nineteenth century – a man is approached by a black dog at Gardner's End crossroads. It vanished after passing him. A number of other people saw it at different times

160. Wheal Eliza Mine: 1984, summer – a woman reports seeing a large black animal three times in this area. It has green, glaring eyes. She does not think it is a cat, but does not specifically say that it is a dog, only that she believes it to be a "disturbed spirit"

161. Whitstone: A black dog was said to haunt the area of Cuttiford Corner at midnight

162. Wistman's Wood: Area said to be haunted by the Whisht Hounds and the Wild Hunt

163. Woolacombe Sands: Legend that the ghost of William de Tracy is said to carry out a penance here spinning ropes of sand. When he has almost finished a black dog appears and breaks the rope with a ball of fire that it carries in its mouth

DORSET

164. Beaminster: 1958 – an old lady saw a black dog with staring eyes and long ears. The dog circled her chair and

she died two months later

165. Bechalwell: It was said to be dangerous to pass a particular gate at night because a black dog used to be there

166. Bridport: 1915 – an old lady reports that she went to church on a Sunday evening and on the way back a black dog as big as a donkey ran past her. When she got home she found that her daughter, who had been ill, had died

167. Burton Bradstock: A black dog is supposed to cross Bredy Lane. Some say that the dog is headless but this is probably a confusion with another nearby account (see Shipton Gorge below)

168. Charmouth: A man reputed to be a white witch saw a black dog which was wearing a chain

169. Chideock: Two people returning from Morcombelake were followed by a large black animal. At the old graveyard at the crossroads to North Chideock and Seatown it walked towards a gravestone and disappeared

170. Deneland: A black dog has been seen near Common Grove

171. Handley: The ghost of a large black dog haunts the Parsonage

172. Harley Gap: The apparition of a pack of old-fashioned foxhounds was seen, in daylight and at night, near Handley Cross

173. Horton: A black dog was reported to cross Pot Lane, running

174. Lyme Regis: 1883 – a man is followed in a quiet lane by a black dog and feels that it is not a natural animal. When he reaches the inn it appears to run through a corner of the building and vanish

175. Manston: A smallish white and yellow dog runs past a woman out for a walk in the evening and disappears

176. Pimperne: Several members of a family are said to have been overtaken by a ghost dog which runs along the Salisbury Road from the bottom of Letton Hill. It has rattling chains but can only be felt and not seen

177. Portland: Legend of the Row Dog, a black dog 'as

high as a man' with fiery eyes 'as big as tea saucers'. Various routes are given for its path of travel. The tale was probably used, though not invented, by smugglers

178. Puncknowle: A black dog with chains is said to jump over a wall on the Swyre to Puncknowle road opposite the end of Hazel Lane. In an alternative version of this account it goes down a lane by Buttery Bars

179. Shipton Gorge: A man met a black dog while he was walking home late at night. He threw a stick at the animal but it passed straight through

180. Shipton Gorge: A legend of a phantom coach at St Catherine's Cross. It is said to be chased by a hound which bays despite being headless

181. Stourpaine: The village square is supposed to be haunted by a black dog. It has a broken chain around its neck and runs through the village to Hod Hill where it disappears. Tradition says that it is the ghost of a real dog which was hit by a horse and cart after running away from its cruel owner

182. Tyneham: A black dog was said to bar the way of people travelling on the Lulworth Road near to Boatswain's Coppice late at night

183. West Woodyates Manor: A man was unloading a cartful of hay when he saw a dog lying amongst it. He used his pitchfork to try and hit it but the dog disappeared in front of him

184. Weymouth: Around the end of the nineteenth century a couple were heading from Weymouth to Dorchester in a trap and were paced by a black dog for part of the journey

185. Woodcutts Priory: Men who used to use the priory ruins to play cards would sometimes see a ghost dog resembling a large black greyhound with huge eyes and no ears run across the room and disappear

186. Yetminster: A large black dog was said to have puts its paws on a woman's shoulders. The location of this account is only stated as possible

DUMBARTONSHIRE

187. Unknown location: A vague story of a doctor in the 1870s who was protected from potential robbers by a black dog which appeared and walked with him

DURHAM

188. Darlington and Stockton Station: A nightwatchman sees a man and a dog in the cellar. The man attacks the witness who fights back but his hand passes through the figure. The dog seizes the nightwatchman's leg and then they both pass into the coal cellar, which has no other door, and vanish

189. Hylton Lane: Tradition of an apparition called the Hylton Lane Brag which appears in various forms including a dog

190. Pilot's Walk: A track by the River Tyne. A woman walking on a stormy night is accompanied by a dog which she feels under her hand

191. Swancliffe: A man is accompanied by a dog which guards him from potential robbers

192. Unknown location: A man reports seeing a dog which is larger than a Newfoundland in a lane. The animal stares at him

ESSEX

193. Alphamstone: 1948 or 1949 – A family at Sycamore Farm were woken by a disturbance in their chicken coup and saw a large grey greyhound. The dog ran off, seemed to pass through the wire, and disappeared

194. Balsham: 1930s – A sighting of a black dog on West Wratting Road at Slough Hill

195. Borley Rectory: 1916-1919 – the occupants of the cottage attached to the rectory frequently hear padding sounds like a dog from the living room adjoining their

bedroom. On the last occasion they hear a crash like china falling but can find nothing out of place.

196. Borley Rectory: 1970s – four people on a ghost watch near the site of the rectory report seeing a phantom greyhound

197. Brentwood: 1968 – A lady who owned a shop which was reputed to be haunted saw a large brown dog jump out of a window into the yard

198. Buckhurst Hill: 1989 – Three teenage boys see a dog in a graveyard.

199. Buckhurst Hill: 1989 – A man driving a car thinks he has hit a dog but it vanishes

200. Butley: 1970s – A man pushing his bike up a hill sees a dog run down the hill towards him. The dog passes straight through him and the bike

201. Chelmsford Area: A local saying here says that someone who is dying has "the black dog at his heel". This refers to the creature as foretelling death

202. Dedham: A ghost of a small black dog appears at Castle House. It is said to be a family pet

203. Dedham: A couple driving on the A12 see a large animal, around the size of a pony. The temperature in the car drops suddenly despite the heater being on

204. Great Warley: The Thatchers' Arms pub is haunted by a black labrador

205. Great Wakering: Tradition of a black dog haunting Star Lane on certain nights. Which nights are referred to is not specified

206. Harwich: There is a fishermen's tradition here that white dogs bring floods. A pack of white dogs were seen running in the harbour prior to the floods of the early 1950s

207. Hatfield Peverell: Legend of 'Shaen's Shaggy Dog' which walked between the gates of a house owned by a family of that name. It was said to be friendly unless annoyed when it brought forth fire

208. Hawkwell: Stories of a large black dog in one of the lanes at this location, near Hockley

209. Hockley: 1958 – A black dog accompanies a lady to the bus stop

210. Hockley: 1965 – A man in a garden sees a large black dog which appeared from nowhere and moved very quickly. Two or three weeks later there was a death in the family

211. Ingrave: August 1967 – A man sees a large brown dog, the size of a Great Dane with 'eyes of fire' at Horse Pond. A week later his brother died, and his wife suffered a brain haemorrhage and died 12 months after the sighting, aged 40

212. Jordan's Green: Someone cycling just after midnight is accompanied by a black dog as far as Seabrook's Lane and sees it again on the return trip. A subsequent search finds that nobody in the area owned a dog matching its description

213. Kelvedon Hatch: A phantom dog, said to be of that belonging to a local poacher whose dog was shot in the church at the start of the 20th century. The animal is said to run around the ruins of the church and enter the porch

214. Lamarsh: Late 1970s – A man hears the footsteps of a dog in his house, Daws Hall, a number of times

215. Manningtree: A man sees a dog running down a hill shortly before a death

216. Manningtree: 1953 – a report of a sighting in the area, but no further details

217. Middleton: A black dog crosses the boundary from Middleton to Boxford, close to Sudbury

218. Mistley: A white dog which appears and runs down Mistley Hill (near Manningtree) is said to presage a death in the Norman family (see entry 215 above for a possible link)

219. Peldon: 1930s – sighting reported on the Wigborough Road

220. Princel House: 1883 – multiple sightings of a white dog

221. Salcott: Two men driving in a horse and trap from Peldon to Guisnes Court see a large black dog with 'eyes like bike lamps' near Salcott crossroads. It follows them for half a mile and suddenly disappears. This may be identical

to entry 219 above.

222. Shoeburyness: A large black dog is said to haunt the lane near the village. No further details

223. Theydon Mount: Just before 1914 – a phantom black dog was sometimes seen in Hill Hall, lying on a bed

224. Tollesbury: Late 20th century – a man travelling from Tolleshunt D'Arcy to Tollesbury sees a large dog with red eyes in the middle of the road. He swerves to avoid hitting it and comes off his motorbike

225. Wigborough: 1946 – a man driving a cart is accompanied by a dog

226. Wigborough Hill: A report of a dog which walks a path between Deldon and Tolleshunt D'Arcy

GLAMORGAN

227. Llancarach: A woman is warned that if she walks over the fields at night she will hear the howling of the hell hound

228. Llyswyrny: Story of a ghost of 'human shape above, but with the body and limbs of a large spotted dog' at a crossroads

229. Morfa: Tradition of the 'Red Dog of Morfa' which would appear underground in a mine before an explosion or disaster

230. Neath District: An old lady who used to cross the mountains in the dark was said to be protected by a white dog

231. Roath: The gallows at the end of Plwcca Lane were said to be haunted by a black dog.

232. Roath: Reference to a location called Bedd y Ci Du (the Black Dog's Grave)

GLOUCESTERSHIRE

233. Alverston: A woman was terrified by a large black dog that crossed her path and would not leave her. She hit at

it with a stick which passed straight through

234. Aust Cliff: Said to be haunted by a pack of hounds which may be the ghosts of those of the Berkeley Hunt who chased a fox over the cliff to their deaths

235. Black Stable Woods: 2004 – A large black dog the size of an alsatian is seen by two women out walking. They thought there was something strange about it (one of them described it as like looking into an 'electric shadow') so took another path

236. Bristol: A large black dog appeared in an inn at the docks in the late 19th century

237. Brockley Combe: A phantom pack of hounds is supposed to run after either a headless horseman or a coach

238. Gatcombe Park: Dozens of people claim to have seen a headless dog on the estate

239. Mickleton: Tradition of a haunting by a dog known as the 'Mickleton Hooter'

240. Minchinhampton: A black dog is said to be seen at Woeful Dane Bottom (site of a battle between the Saxons and the Danes

241. Minchinhampton: Reports of a black dog near the Long Stone at Gatcombe (close to a long barrow)

242. Moreton-in-the-Marsh: A black dog is said to come along the lane at this location. Some people say that there are two dogs

243. Northwick Road: A number of sightings of a black dog between Northwick House and the White Horse pub

244. Stroud Area: A black dog accompanies a minister despite his trying to get rid of it. Later on his journey he passes two unsavoury looking men, after which the dog disappears

245. Tetbury: Two women see a black dog on its own in a field for a period of minutes and think it strange. One of these was also the witness at Black Stable Woods (entry 235 above)

246. Winchcombe: A man walking at night sees another man with a dog. They seem to pass through a closed gate

247. Woodchester Priory: A black dog was seen many times in a lane near the priory. It often accompanied the Prior

GUERNSEY

248. Buttes Road: Story of a boy fetching medicine for his grandfather being accompanied by a black dog. He hits at it with a stick and the dog vanishes. On returning home he finds his grandfather died at the time that the dog vanished

249. Clos du Valle: To see a black dog here is said to be a sign of a death to follow

250. Hougue Hatenez: There is said to be a black dog in the forest, but sometimes only chains can be heard. Sometimes thought of as a death portent

251. La Bete de la Devise de Saumarez a St Martin: A black dog is said to haunt the avenue by the manor

252. La Rue de la Bete: Said to be haunted by a black dog the size of a calf

253. La Ville Baudu: A black dog said to be seen at this location is considered unlucky

254. St Andrews: A black dog with chains haunted the Forest Road. It was said to be the spirit of a bailiff hanged in 1320

HAMPSHIRE

255. Abbotts Ann: Reports that a large black dog is sometimes seen near here

256. Lymington: A black dog runs through a room and vanishes in a place where there is no egress as a woman is telling her children that if they are not good "Tyrrell's Dog" would come for them

257. New Forest: A man working tells another that the ghost of a small white dog runs howling from a house at certain times. A man once hanged himself in the house

258. Odiham: Reports of a ghostly dog in the fields

between here and North Wanborough

259. Petersfield: A man is accompanied by a black dog for a period before it melts away

260. Winchester: Scant reports of a black dog attached to Symond's Street, which used to be called Dog Walk

HEBRIDES

261. Tiree: Locals on this island report frequent sightings of a black dog. Most sightings are around the area of the beach. The dog, which has a hollow bark, is said to follow people before disappearing

262. Various: Tradition of ghost dog called The Lamper which was large and white, with no tail. It normally ran in circles and foretold a death. One man reported seeing it and hitting it with his stick, which passed through, on the day before his father died

HEREFORDSHIRE

263. Clodock: A dog was reported to appear in the lane about half a mile below Clodock Church at a particular cottage. It would follow horses and other vehicles for a while before disappearing

264. Cusop: A lawyer defending a man accused of murdering his wife is confronted at her grave by a mongrel dog and cannot approach. Nobody else who visits the grave ever has trouble getting near it

265. Hampton Court Castle: It is said that tragedy will come to anybody who removed the painting of a dog, called the Coningsbury Hound, from the castle.

266. Hergest: A black dog is associated with Hergest Court and is linked with a man called Vaughan who was killed in 1469. Some believe this case is the inspiration for Conan Doyle's Baskerville family

267. Little Cowarne: 1986 - A woman sees a dog cross the road close to the church and disappear

Appendix

HERTFORDSHIRE

268. Stevenage: A black dog which haunts an old lane leading to the parish church is said to be a guardian which patrols the boundary of the church at night

269. Stevenage: Two women waiting at the church at about 11pm one night see a black dog run past them. It is the size of a calf

270. Stevenage: A lady reports seeing a large dog which has curly looking fur

271. Tring: A black dog is said to haunt a spot where a man was hung. Two people witnessed it disappear by seeming to sink into the ground

272. Tring: A man returning late from the station saw a dog which he described as "like a St Bernard". He tried to stroke it but his hand passed straight through

HUNTINGDONSHIRE

273. Fens: Tradition of a black dog coming out of the fens to warn members of the Allpress family about an impending tragedy

274. Ramsey Heights: A black dog is associated with a road on one of the islands, on a gravel ridge with fen on either side

INVERNESS

275. Arisaig: A large shaggy dog with red eyes is said to haunt the woods. It is known locally as Cu Glas (Gaelic for grey dog)

276. Arisaig: A black dog was said to appear at the time that a member of the Macdonald (or Clan Ranald) family died

276. Claggan: A ghost which haunted the area of the farmhouse, south of Loch Tay, sometimes took the form of a dog

277. Creag an Ordain: A black dog is said to be seen to several people on the road to Lochinver from Stoer Sutherland

278. Murthley: Near Douglasfield – legend of a dog which guards treasure buried under a stone at a mound

IRELAND

279. Arvagh: A black dog is said to haunt the drive of Holly Bank House. The apparition alternates with a lady in white. Horses are said not to pass through the spot

280. Bunratty: A black dog is regularly seen outside a farmhouse where in the 1950s the farmer is said to have bulldozed a faery fort

281. Clare: A black dog jumping from a coffin in a grave features in the story of 'Leeam O'Rooney's Burial'

282. Doolin: Story of a man seeing a large black dog when out walking near the fort. The dog is said to disappear

283. Dublin: St Patrick's Cathedral is reputed to be haunted by the ghost of a dog.

284. Fermanagh: Legend of St Patrick removing two hounds which emit fire from their mouths, nostrils and eyes. Said to be the etymology behind a place name of 'Hound's Mouth'

285. Londonderry: 1928 – A college student sees a black dog with red eyes by the river

286. Lough Conn: 1930s – a black dog was seen at Pontoon Bridge, which joins Lough Conn and Lough Cullin. Two sightings are possibly recorded

287. Rockabill: Legend that the Rockabill islands were formed by the two halves of a dog whose mistress was worshipped as a river goddess

288. Templeogue: A woman walking with a serving maid sees a black dog cross the path at Pussy's Leap, accompanied by the sound of chains. The maid can hear the chains but does not see the dog

Appendix

ISLE OF MAN

289. Castletown: There is a report that people are pulled off their horses here by black dogs but the reference is very vague

290. Peel: Tradition that black dogs are seen at the full moon

291. Peel: Story that a woman who is walking to see a local witch for a charm is attacked by men but saved by a black dog which appears and has been sent by the witch

292. Peel Castle: Haunted by a black dog with curly hair (usually described as a spaniel), called the Mauthe Doog

ISLE OF WIGHT

293. Western area: A man driving reports that he hits a black dog which disappears

JERSEY

294. Cinq Verges: A black dog was reported to run from Ville au Neveu to Cinq Verges. It had a chain hanging from its neck

295. Petit Port: There was said to be a house where a black dog guarded treasure at a location where the railway crosses to road. A modern house now stands on the site

KENT

296. Chilham: 1947 – a man reports seeing a dog cross a track which is close to a barrow

297. Goodhurst: 1950s – a woman sleeping in the oldest part of the village school building wakes up and sees an animal crouching in the corner of the room and staring at her. It does so for some hours. Not described specifically as a dog

298. Leeds Castle: Said to be haunted by a grey lady

accompanied by a black dog in some reports. Seen by a housekeeper in the 1940s

299. Leeds Castle: A retriever-type dog was said to appear, foretelling disaster, for the old owners of the castle

300. Smarden: 1995 – four people out driving stop in fog and while stopped they see a dog walk past which is described as being as big as the car

301. Trottiscliffe: (pronounced Trosley) A ghostly hound is sighted a few times in woods near to the Pilgrims Way

302. Unknown location: A woman suffering from a blood infection sees a small black dog during a stressful night. She recovers soon afterwards

303. Westerham: 1960 – A man on a motorbike is paced for some yards by a large dog

304. Westerham: Local tradition that if you see the black dog with a child then you will die within the year, from some form of ritual murder

LAKE DISTRICT

305. Cappleside Hill: Legend that the hill is named after a black dog with red eyes called the Cappel which lived in a barn at the now demolished Cappleside Hall

306. Levens: A black dog runs out in front of visitors before disappearing at Levens Hall. Reports of sightings from 1958 and 1973 among others

LANCASHIRE

307. Accrington: 1980s – a group of school friends see a dog at the disused power station

308. Askam in Furness: Local saying that "if a black dog follows you, comes near you and won't run away, it is a sure sign of a death"

309. Bradshaw: A young soldier sees a dog. When he touches the animal it leaps into the air and vanishes

310. Burnley: Tradition of the black dog in this area

referred to as the Trash or Skriker. Said to be a death omen

311. Chipping: Story of a man sighting a black dog on a couple of occasions. Following this his son is drowned, his wife dies of a chill and he becomes mad

312. Clayworth: 1594 – Old story of a possession case which includes a woman seeing a black dog with a monstrous tail and a long chain

313. Dobb Park Lodge: Legend of a man who is set a trial in the underground passages by a black dog in order to gain a treasure

314. Formby Beach: A black dog with luminous eyes which is said to bring bad luck or death to anyone seeing it. Multiple sightings are recorded

315. Godley Green: Reports of a ghostly brown dog being seen in many parts of Godley Green. One man tried to touch it but his hand passed straight through the animal

316. Holden: An old woman is accompanied by a dog which vanishes in a burst of flame

317. Manchester: 1819 – A man is accompanied by a dog which protects him from two men before disappearing

318. Manchester: 1825 – A headless black dog appears outside the Old Church and forces a man to run home by placing its paws on his shoulders. It was exorcised under the bridge over the River Irwell

319. Manchester: 1996 – Two people run over a dog in Manchester City Centre and the animal vanishes

320. Manchester: 2002 – Two people see a dog walk through the wall of a building

321. Radcliffe Tower: Haunted by a black dog said to be the ghost of a cook who murdered a woman and turned her into a meat pie

322. Rochdale: A black dog is said to haunt in the thrutch between sunset and sunrise

323. Stannicliffe: A house was said to be haunted by a ghost which appeared in various forms including a black dog

324. Shirebank Hall: Haunted by a black dog with curly

hair which used to foretell a death by howling

325. Thackergate: A phantom dog was said to come out of a pit at night

326. Unknown location: A black dog with fiery eyes, known as 'Spalding's Dog' is frequently seen

327. Wycollar Hall: An apparition of the old squire is said to appear, accompanied by a ghostly dog

LEICESTERSHIRE

328. Ab Kettleby: 1930s – a couple see a dog which presages the death of a family member

329. Ab Kettleby: 1940s – a woman reports seeing a snarling dog. Shortly afterwards her husband is killed fighting in the war

330. Anstey: A ghost dog known as the Shag-Dog is said to have haunted a lane in the area

331. Stoney Stanton: 1809 – a man hears a groaning noise shortly before a shaggy dog rushes past him on a bridge

LINCOLNSHIRE

332. Algakirk: A woman reports seeing a dog run out from a group of trees

333. Barrow on Humber: 1983 – a woman driving sees a dog cross the road in front of her car

334. Barton: 1912 – a woman is accompanied by a dog which protects her from a tramp before it disappears

335. Burton Stather: 1937 – a man cycling is accompanied by a dog

336. Caythorpe: 1920s – a man cycling alongside a wall is accompanied by a dog which subsequently disappears

337. Crosby: A woman is accompanied by a dog which protects her from some suspicious looking men before it disappears

338. Grayingham: A woman sees a dog which she tries to hit her with umbrella, but it passes straight through

339. Kesteven: A man and a woman walking through a wood are accompanied by a dog

340. Kirton: 1900s – a nurse sees a dog which speaks to her

341. Kirton: 1935 – a woman sees a dog walk around the kitchen of her farmhouse

342. Leverton: 1890s – a dog is reported to accompany a man

343. Manton: a woman out cycling is accompanied by a dog

344. Manston: 1935 – a pedestrian sees a dog lying on a culvert by the side of the road

345. Scawby: 1940 – a dog crosses the road in front of somebody out cycling

346. South Kelsey: a woman sees a dog walking along which suddenly disappears

347. Spilsby: A variety of reports of a ghost dog known as the 'White Dog of Eresby'

348. Swaby: 1900s – a woman is accompanied by a dog as far as a bridge, before it vanishes

349. Swaby: 1950s – A woman out walking hears feet scratching around her, like a dog

350. Ulceby: 1977 – a dog runs out in front of a woman driving and she has to brake to avoid hitting it. The dog then vanishes

351. Unknown location: 1922 or 1923 – A man out making deliveries sees a pair of eyes in front of him on the path, at a spot reputed to be haunted. They remain for a while before "blotting out". He thinks that the dog from a nearby dairy has followed him, but upon checking it is not the case

352. Unknown location: A man is accompanied for a time by a dog which then vanishes

353. Unknown location: 1982 – a passenger in a lorry sees a black dog walking in the road. It stopped and turned its head but seemed to have no features and just look like a vivid shadow. It subsequently disappeared. The witness heard a report on the radio some years later than someone

else had had a sighting in the same area

354. West Halton: 1933 – a man out cycling has a dog run alongside him. It keeps up regardless of the pace of the bike

355. West Stockwith: A woman reports seeing a dog go into her house

356. Willoughby: A Methodist preacher is accompanied by a dog through some woods

357. Willoughton: 1900s – a man out cycling sees a dog cross the road in front of him

358. Willoughton: 1910s – A woman is accompanied by a black dog both to her destination and on the way back

359. Willoughton: 1933 – a man reports being forced up against a post by an invisible dog

360. Willoughton: 1934 – an Irish labourer has a dog accompany him along a stretch of road

361. Willoughton: a man hears a dog come through a hedge, accompanied by the sound of crackling

362. Willoughton: A man sees a dog disappear with a loud noise. The incident takes place on a curve in the road, next to a tree

363. Wrawby: 1976 – a man reports being jumped on by a dog while he is asleep

LONDON

364. Kensington: Late 1800s – a child has recurring dreams involving a black dog at Ghuznee House

365. Maida Vale: Before the First World War – a woman and her daughters experience cries and see a black dog in a room at their flat, which used to be a nursing home.

MERIONETH

366. Harlech: A yellow dog would appear to a family at a Tudor house called Maesyneuarrd to foretell a death. A witness saw it on the lawn in the early morning before the deaths of her mother and brother

Appendix

MIDLOTHIAN

367. Edinburgh: A house in Mary King's Close had various hauntings including a large dog which jumped on a chair and vanished. Attempts by the clergy failed to quieten the house and it was pulled down as tenants could not be found for it

NORFOLK

368. Attlebridge: A sighting is recorded in the 1890s but there are no further details

369. Bacton: Two fishermen who owned a large black dog between them were drowned at sea along with their pet. The ghost of the dog was said to run between their two graves

370. Bacton: 1982 – a woman drives past a dog which she says has one glowing eye

371. Barnby: 1968 – a man reports seeing a dog with a chain

372. Bawburgh: A man says that his life is saved by a dog which is hit by a car driving down the road with no lights. The car appeared to hit the dog, but after it passed the animal was still there

373. Beeston: A traditional account exists of a black dog on the road to Bacton

374. Beeston: A black dog is said to rise out of the sea here, but there are no further details

375. Bexwell: An account of a sighting in the 19th century on the road to Downham. No further details

376. Blickling Hall: A legend of a Shuck type black dog which emerges from the mouth of a fish that is caught in a lake near the Hall

377. Buxton Lamas Church: 1930 – A man is walking near the church when a large dog appears at his side. He goes to pat it but it has already disappeared. The following week he receives a letter that says that his brother died at the time he saw the dog

378. Catfield: 1842 – report of a dog being seen on the

marshes. No further information

379. Cley: 1968 – eyewitness account of a dog seen at the bottom of Cley Hill

380. Coltishall: A headless dog is said to cross the bridge here each night

381. Coltishall: 1897 – a man who has already had an sighting at Neatishead Lane (see below) is paced by a dog which he says has the glint of fiery eyes despite being headless

382. Coltishall: Two people hear a dog pass them on the bridge

383. Cromer: Two schoolboys see a large black animal near the railway bridge

384. Cromer: 19th century – multiple sightings of a black dog on the clifftop

385. Cromer: 19th century – report of a dog seen close to the lighthouse

386. Cromer: A man who sees a black dog tries to hit it with a stick but it passes straight through

387. Diss: 1897 – A man and woman sitting on a stile see a large black dog that looks like it wants to go over the stile. They jump off to let it over but it vanishes

388. Ditchingham: The black dog of Bungay was seen here on the Norfolk side of the River Waveney according to a tradition recorded by Rider Haggard

389. Ditchingham: 1938 – A man sees a dog approach him and then vanish

390. East Dereham: 1945 – A man out cycling is followed by a dog which then disappears

391. East Flegg: A black dog is said to haunt the churchyards in this area. An old tradition says that the ground it crossed would become scarred as if it had been on fire

392. Flegg: One man out of two who are walking together sees a dog. This man later dies

393. Foxley: 1602 – a vague report of a sighting but no further details

394. Garvestone: A ghostly dog said to be the size of a

pony with blazing eyes was said to haunt the lanes in this area. It always disappeared in the same lane, which is not stated

395. Garvestone: Late 1970s – A man walking during the day saw a dog about 20 yards ahead of him. He looked away briefly at another walker and when he looked back the dog had gone despite there being no cover for it to have gone into

396. Geldeston: A huge dog, described as a hell hound, is traditionally reported in this area, particularly at a clump of trees called the Gelders near to the Beccles Road

397. Geldeston: 1901 – A man out walking is followed by a dog which keeps the same pace as him. When he eventually turns to look he sees it is of a large size with fearsome looking eyes. When he reached the churchyard it seemed to run through the wall

398. Gorleston: 1800s – A man out walking met a dog with rattling chains. When he told it to go it threw him over a hedge

399. Gorleston: A woman twice sees an animal like a dog, but with longer legs, on two streets in Gorleston

400. Gorleston: 1972 – A coastguard sees a large black dog on the beach at daybreak and it vanishes while he is watching it

401. Great Yarmouth: 1800s – A woman out at night meets a large black dog which appears out of the darkness. It puts its paws on her shoulders and she can smell its noxious breath

402. Great Yarmouth: 19th century – report of a sighting near South Town railway station. No further details

403. Great Yarmouth: 19th century – report of a sighting at Blackfriars Road. No further details

404. Great Yarmouth: 19th century – report of a sighting at Quayhead. No further details

405. Hemby: 1996 – a man sees a fierce looking dog in the road

406. Hempnall: 1930s – A man sees a dog which looks

like it is about to cross in front of the bike he is riding, but instead the dog vanishes

407. Hethersett: Traditional account of a black dog in Mill Road

408. Hethersett: 1890s – A man passes a dog with large eyes. The animal is picked up by a gust of wind

409. Hilgay: 1945 – A witness hears the baying of a dog in the distance. The sound gets louder and reaches a crescendo and they hear a noise like a chain being dragged on the road. The location is close to a bridge over the River Wissey

410. Irstead: A man kicks out at a dog in the road but his foot passes straight through the animal

411. Lenwade: 1890s – vague report of a sighting but no further details

412. Long Stratton: Vague report of a sighting but no details or date

413. Lyng: 1890s – vague report of a sighting but no further details

414. Magdalen: 1865 – a man dies after seeing a dog coming towards his cottage. He was said to be scared to death

415. Manea: 1941 – eyewitness account of a sighting on the river bank close to the bridge

416. Marshland: A dog crosses the road in front of a horse and cart and scares the horse

417. Mautby: Vague reference to a sighting but with no date or location details

418. Morston: early 20th century – eyewitness account of a sighting on the road to Blackeney

419. Neatishead Lane: 1897 – a man is followed by a dog for about quarter of a mile but when he turned to look at it, it had vanished

420. Norwich: Tradition of a black dog called the Skutch

421. Overstrand: A lane in the parish is known as Shuck's Lane

422. Overstrand: late 19th century – A man is followed by

a dog and when he tries to hit it with a stick it passes straight through

423. Peddar's Way: A black Shuck-like dog is said to haunt this road

424. Ranworth: A large black dog is said to guard treasure buried by monks from a nearby priory at Ranworth Hall

425. Rockland: 1893 – Two men were driving along a lane when their path was blocked by a dog. They drove on and as the cart hit it the air became full with flame and a sulpherous smell

426. Salhouse: Tradition of a black dog with one fiery eye in the middle of its forehead

427. Salthouse: early 20th century – report of a sighting on the marshes

428. Salthouse: A man sees a dog which walks through a closed gate

429. Salthouse: A man is followed home by a dog which howls. When a gun is fired at it the bullets pass straight through

430. Sheringham: A black dog is said to haunt the coast in this area

431. Sheringham: 1960s – a dog accompanies a man out cycling. He can hear its chain on the ground

432. Sheringham: A farmer sees a dog which crosses the road and appears to go through a closed gate

433. Sidestrand: A woman out walking sees a black dog which walks past her and vanishes when she turns round to look at it

434. Southery: 1941 – eyewitness account of a sighting on the main road, close to the river bridge

435. South Lopham: Two women coming out the church see a black dog sitting in the rain. One of them believes that the dog travels back with them 'in spirit'. She dies a few weeks later

436. Stiffkey: early 19th century – tradition of a dog haunting the salt marshes between Wells and Blakeney

437. Stiffkey: 1920s – A man is followed by a howling

dog. He hides in a cottage to lose it

438. Stiffkey: A man was reported to have had his throat torn out by a dog

439. Swanton Morley: 1945 – report of a haunting on the road near the RAF camp

440. "T" Hall: A witness sees a dog on three occasions at Bluebell Wodd, close to the Hall (which is not named). On the first two it runs alongside their bike. On the third it is seen in front of a friend's bike, but the friend doesn't see it

441. Tasburgh: 19th century – report of a sighting on the road to Flordon railway station

442. Thetford: 1977 – A woman staying at a house in Magdalen Street wakes up and sees a man standing horizontally above her. He has a black dog sitting next to him.

443. Thetford Bridge: 1800s – An invisible dog tries to push a blind boy and his sister into the river

444. Unknown location: 1910s – a boy out on an errand sees a dog and later dies

445. Waxham: 1979 – Four schoolgirls camping on a beach hear breathing, footsteps and movement outside their tent. They believe it is a Shuck

446. West Runton: Early 20th century – eyewitness account of a sighting on the road to Overstrand

447. West Runton: 1972 – eyewitness account of a sighting near the slipway at the foot of a cliff

448. Wicken Burwell: Vague reference to a sighting but no date or further details

449. Winfarthing: A woman saw a large black dog approaching her cottage. It walked up to the gate and disappeared. Shortly afterwards her grandfather died

450. Yarmouth: Tradition of a black dog known as Scarfe on the banks of the river Yare and at the Southtown Road. Sometimes took the form of a black goat

NORTHAMPTONSHIRE

451. Whittlebury and Rockingham: Tradition of a pack of hell hounds in these areas

NORTHUMBERLAND

452. Black Heddon: A servant alone in a house saw something black fall from the ceiling which turned out to be a large dog's skin filled with gold

453. Blenkinsopp Hall: A dog is said to appear here as a warning of a death

454. Blyth: Two people report seeing a dog in a cemetery. The animal turns into a blanket of mist and floats away

455. Broomley: A girl in her teens out walking is protected from two tramps in the woods by a black dog which then disappears

456. Hexamshire Common: A black dog at a former monastery called Blanchard is said to foretell death

457. Newcastle: The streets were said to be haunted by a dog in the shape of a mastiff with huge eyes

458. Northumberland coast: A man on a dangerous footpath leading to a cave is guided by a black dog which later disappears

NOTTINGHAMSHIRE

459. Blyth Road: 1991 – A woman driving near Hodsock Priory in the early hours of the morning sees a black dog larger than a Great Dane which looks like it is dragging something across the road

460. Bunting Nock: Crossroads said to be haunted by a black dog

461. North Muskham: 1915 – A man frequently sees a black dog at Crow Lane in the same place that his grandfather was often accompanied by a black dog

ORKNEY

462. Hoy: 1970 – a woman on holiday with her family in a cottage sees a black dog come into the house and disappear in front of her eyes. Later in the holiday everyone is woken by a loud crash but can find no cause. A few weeks later the woman's mother dies

463. Quholm: A large dog is said to emerge from under a bridge across the road to Sandwick and Birsay and follow people for a distance before disappearing.

464. Quholm: A young boy walking across a field sees a dog which grows in front of him into a large object and follows him to his destination.

OXFORD

465. Culworth: 1988 – a man riding a motorbike on the Culworth Road sees a black animal with red eyes come out of a barn and run alongside him briefly on several occasions

466. Fritwell: A dog is seen which runs alongside cyclists. One man tried to pat it, but found that there was no substance to it

467. Headington: A report of a dog with saucer eyes in Barton Lane

468. Leafield: Tradition of a black dog which haunts the churchyard, jumps over the wall and runs away northwards

469. Old Marston: 1954 or 1955 – a woman is believed to have seen a black dog here

470. Thame: 1960s – a dog ghost was reported twice, but no further details

471. Westwell: A dog ghost is reported to disappear into a drain near the manor. It is said to be the ghost of a dog that once belonged to the keeper there

472. Wilscote: A black dog is said to have been laid here by a clergyman

473. Woodstock: 1649 – tradition of a dog ghost appearing in the bedchamber of two commissioners and their servants in connection with their cutting down of an old oak tree

PEMBROKESHIRE

474: Brymbo: Multiple accounts of an apparition named the Beast of Brymbo which exhibits some black dog characteristics

475. Cot-Moor Field: A man walking across a field sees a dog which, when he tries to throw a stone at it, becomes surrounded by fire

476. Haverfordwest: A black dog haunts the road between here and Pembroke Ferry. There are multiple reports of sightings

477. Haycastle: Folk tale of a black dog attached to an ancient family

478. Redhill: 1830s – A man walking by a bridge sees a large black dog rise over the trees and swoop down in front of him with a roar

PERTHSHIRE

479. Ballinluigh: 19th century – the head of the house said that when he died his soul would pass into his favourite black spaniel and so it was destroyed upon his death. For a time afterwards a dog was often smelt in the castle

480. Blairgowrie: Legend of a man being earthbound in the form of a grey dog

481. Murthly: Legend that anyone who can move a large standing stone will find a treasure chest guarded by a black dog

POWYS

482. Caersws: A black dog the size of a bull is said to frighten horses near Maesmawr

483. Carreghova: People travelling from Pant to Llanymynech make a detour to avoid a spot said to be haunted by a black dog

484. Castle Caereinion: 1878 – report of a black dog sighting

485. Crossgates: A mile north of Crossgates on the A483 a black dog was said to appear from a hedge, dragging a piece of broken chain

486. Cyfronydd: Report of a woman sighting a black dog

487. Llandysilio: The ghost of a black dog was sometimes seen close to a quarry

488. Meifod: Tradition of a black dog appearing at certain times of the year

SARK

489. Tchico: Tradition of a ghost dog which is sometimes said to be black, and sometimes white

SCILLY ISLES

490. St Mary's: Legend of a tunnel connecting with Tresco where dogs which go in one end emerge at the other with most of their hair burned off

SHROPSHIRE

491. Baschurch: 1997 – two men driving a van swerve to miss a large black dog which stands in the middle of the road and does not move. When they go back to look it has disappeared

492. Church Stretton: People are said to feel and sometimes smell a ghostly dog at a certain corner where, 40 years previously, a black dog was sighted

SOMERSET

493. Bardon: Tradition of a black dog in this area which is widely known of

494. Bishop's Lydears: A ghost dog was heard in an upstairs corridor at the Old Forge on a number of occasions, but only seen once

495. Blackdown: A black dog haunts a lane where there used to be a Roman lookout post

496. Blackdown Barrows: Tradition of a haunting by black dogs, but no confirmation

497. Bucknoller: An elderly lady walking her dog is joined by a black dog which her own pet does not seem to notice. It then disappears

498. Bud Leigh Hill: 1907 – report of a sighting of a black dog with large fiery eyes

499. Chard: A black dog is said to haunt a tunnel where the road passes underneath the railway

500. Chaffcombe: 1914-1918 – a woman sees a dog prior to her son being killed in the war

501. Clevedon: A dog looking like a brown mongrel is said to haunt the Copse Road

502. Combwich: Folk tale of a disbelieving man being met by a ghostly carriage pulled by a gold pig and accompanied by a black dog

503. Crowcombe: Multiple stories of a black dog in this area

504. Dulverton: Belief in a black dog which guards the churchyard and approaches from the north side

505. East Harptree: An apparition is reported to appear at Fair Ash Crossroads and travel to Stonystyle Pool where it disappeared. Variously described as a dog, a calf or a cat

506. Edithmead: A black dog was said to haunt a lane. A clicking sound and the noise of a chain always came before its appearance and it would turn into fire before disappearing

507. Exford: 1978 – a couple driving see a dog with white hair staring at their car. Later there is an associated death

508. Kingsdon: 1898 – A woman walking on a country road sees a black dog the size of a colt

509. Langford Budville: Traditions of a black dog haunting this area

510. Langport: Traditions of a black dog in this area and many place names are associated with it

511. Mendip: 1870s – tradition of a witch in this area who could take the form of a black dog

512. Perry Hill: 1930s – a black dog was seen by a courting couple. The girl died within a year of the sighting

513. Porlock: Two sightings of a black dog with which a death are associated quickly afterwards

514. Quantock Hills: Multiple reports of black dog sightings

515. Quantockshead: Belief that a black dog haunts the sea road between Staple and Perry Farm

516. Rodway Hill: Folk tale that an unbeliever who jeered at a priest was brushed up against by a black dog and paralysed

517. Sampford Common: 1963 – a man sees a black dog with a chain. He believes it to be a farm dog and tries to lead it off but it fades away

518. Selworthy: 1847 – a woman sees a dog run past her and then disappear in a ball of fire

519. Selworthy: Reports of a black dog haunting at the crossroads

520. Standwick: A black dog is said to haunt a lane

521. Stapley: Tradition of a black dog appearing as black, white or grey as a death omen. Report of being seen by a man before a death, but his sister who was also there did not see it

522. St Audries: A black dog tradition haunting a road between here and Perry Farm. The dog is said to be a death omen

523. Street House: Two brothers saw a large white dog sitting opposite their stove. Three weeks later their father died

524. Stogursey: A black dog was said to rush out from a witch-tree and was believed to be a shape changing witch

525. Thorne St Margaret: The Devil was said to live in a cottage at a meadow called Bug Hole in the 17th century in the form of a dog

526. Tickenham: A large dog is said to cross the main

road and walk through the wall on the opposite side

527. Unknown location: A black dog was said to come into a man's garden at dusk and also accompany him when walking at night but if he ever tried to pat it, then it would disappear

528. Upton Noble: A man walking up Gold Hill was said to have met a small boy who turned into a large black dog before disappearing through the Rectory gates

529. Weacombe: A man lost in fog is guided home by a dog that he can feel next to him, although he cannot see it

530. Wells: A stone outside 18 Tor Street has a coloured relief of a black dog, dated 1562. The building used to be an inn

531. Wembarrow: A dog was said to be seen by people out hunting if they rode too close to the cairn

532. Winsford Hill: A saucer-eyed dog was said to be seen which if watched faded away leaving only its eyes which then diminish. Last reported seen in the 1940s

533. Worle Hill: A witch during the 19th century was said to have turned herself into a snarling dog and bit a man

STAFFORDSHIRE

534. Bradnop: A black dog haunts the road at Oxhay Farm where there is a Jacobite grave

535. Ipstones: 1916 – a black dog was seen near to Hermitage Farm which is said to be haunted

536. Ipstones: A black dog is seen in association with Indefont Well

537. Kidgrew Bugget: The name of a black dog which is seen before a mining disaster in Staffordshire. Possibly a corruption of Kisgrove which is in the heart of the mining area

538. Kidsgrove: 1886 – Two people hear a dog running towards them but cannot see anything

539. Kidsgrove: 1895 – a Diglake Colliery miner is followed from the pit by a black dog which disappears. This

precedes a disaster at the mine (see entry 537 above)

540. Kidsgrove: 1939 – a man reports being accompanied by a dog

541. Kidsgrove: 1940s – a man hears the sound of a dog running alongside him

542. Kidsgrove: 1945 – a woman is followed by a light coloured dog. There is a fire in the area shortly afterwards

543. Leek: 1896 – A man is prevented from crossing a bridge by a dog which growls at him

544. Leek: 1920s – Two women are followed by a dog which subsequently vanishes

545. Leek: A woman is frightened by meeting a strange dog

546. Mow Cop: A policeman sees a dog which appears to run through the churchyard gate

547. Mucklow Hill: A greyhound is said to walk by a pool near Stone where there was a suicide

548. Swinscow: A black dog is said to guard a grave on the Leek-Ashburne road

STIRLINGSHIRE

549. Stirling Castle: 1938 – A woman and her son visiting the castle are accompanied for a long period of time by a black dog

SUFFOLK

550. Aldeburgh: A large house near the church was said to be haunted by a headless dog which passes through a small bedroom

551. Aldeburgh: 1891 – a man is attacked by a dog when walking in a tree-lined avenue

552. Barham: Shortly before World War I – two men are followed by a large dog with glowing eyes. One tries to hit it with a stick which passes through the animal and hits a wall

553. Barnby: Multiple sightings of a black dog at a place

called Water Bars. In many the dog is headless

554. Barnby: Two women walking at a location where the stream flows under the road see a black dog. They try to catch it but it shrinks to the size of a cat and disappears

555. Blythburgh: 1557 – legend that a black dog attacked the church during a storm after having done the same at Bungay (see below)

556. Blythburgh: Some stretches of the old rail line are said to be haunted by a Shuck-like dog

557. Bungay: 1577 – legend that a black dog attacked the church during a storm

558. Bungay: 1917 – a woman sees a dog which appears to pass through the churchyard door

559. Bungay: 1950s – a woman sees a dog run across a street and then disappear

560. Bungay: 1970 – A woman reports a dog running past her at the time that her sister dies

561. Bungay: Black dog sightings reported in Earsham Road

562. Bungay: Black dog sightings reported in Broad Street

563. Bungay: Black dog sightings reported in Trinity Street

564. Bungay: Black dog sightings reported in Bigod Way

565. Bungay: 2004 – a woman reports seeing a wolf-like dog with red eyes which runs towards the church

566. Burgh: 1823 – a phantom white dog is said to haunt a boggy pool called Bath Slough

567. Clopton: An apparition with the body of a monk and the head of a dog is said to guard treasure

568. Clopton Green: 19th century – a man sees an animal with saucer eyes on the road to Woolpit on the night before he died. The creature grew in size and said "I shall want you within a week"

569. Corton: A black dog is said to walk Tramps Alley at night

570. Debach: Early 20th century – a dog is said to haunt an unspecified road

571. Ditchingham: Multiple reports of sightings at Hollow Hill

572. Dunwich Abbey: The ruins are said to be haunted by a black dog

573. Earsham: 1920s – a man sees a dog walk across the road and pass through a wall

574. Farnham: A black dog is seen twice in a house in West Street and there are multiple other sightings

575. Felixstowe: A legend of an Italian sorcerer who turned into a black dog and attacked a boy. In some accounts the story is placed at Lowestoft

576. Halesowen: 1929 – a woman sights a dog and the following day a row of cottages burns down

577. Harwich: Early 1950s – reported sighting at the harbour and quayside

578. Ipswich: 1970s – A ten year old boy sleeping in a house in Coniston Square wakes up and sees a "plum pudding" dog on his bed. Some weeks later bones are found in the garden which appear to belong to a Dalmatian which was owned by the neighbours

579. Leiston: A black dog known as Galley Trot is said to haunt the coast and was seen in a churchyard at midnight

580. Lowestoft: A man sees a dog which appears shortly before a fishing boat sinks and all the crew are killed

581. Melton: A man was reported to have seen an animal with the head of a donkey and the body of a dog sitting on a tollgate near the Horse and Groom Inn.

582. Newmarket: 1983 – A man in bed in a house in Park Avenue hears a dog come up the stairs and into his room, but when he turns the light on there is nothing there and the door is still closed

583. Oulton: A tradition of a black dog on the marshes, but no further details

584. Sizewell: 1982 – Two people walking near Sizewell Hall see a black dog running alongside a car travelling at about 30mph. After the car passes they look again and the dog has vanished

585. South Tuckswood: 1986 – A man reports seeing a

large dog with red eyes which jumps over a wall in his yard

586. Southwold: Mid 20th century – multiple sightings by two people of a black dog in various rooms at Squires Tearoom

587. Southwold: The ghost of a woman and her dog are said to haunt a lane between South Green and Skilman's Hill

588. Southwold: 1900s – Two people see a dog which vanishes while they are out driving in their cart

589. Stoke-by-Clare: 1950s – A male witness on holiday at the 'old Elwes house' sees and is followed by a black dog multiple times over two days. He refuses to ever go back to the house, which has a reputation for being haunted

590. St Olaves: 1939 – a man sees a dog with lamp-like eyes. His own dog is scared by it

591. Unknown location: A woman on holiday in an 18th century barn conversion is woken by crackling noises and sees a large black dog which lies on the bed between herself and her husband

592. Unknown location: A man is reported to hear the noise of a dog pass him on a road

593. Walberswick: A traditional account of a black dog at Tinkers Barn on the marshes

594. Walberswick: A woman on the beach sees a black dog floating around her own dog. A local lady tells her it is the ghost of a dog called Chuff

595. Walberswick: 1940s – An American soldier reports hearing and seeing a dog attacking his house at night

596. Walberswick: A report of two women seeing a dog

597. Walberswick: A report of a witness seeing a dog in a lane

598. Woodbridge: A white dog is said to haunt this area, also known as Galley Trot (see entry 579 above)

SURREY

599. Unknown location: A man working on a farm fires

a gun at a black dog with red eyes which has been banging on his trailer

SUSSEX

600. Alfriston: A woman sees a dog cross a field, look over a wall and then run back

601. Bexhill: A girl aged 5 sees a black dog often in the garden of her house. Twenty years later as a parent living in Scotland her own daughter (aged around 2) wakes up and says that she sees a black dog in the garden. Both dogs have differing colour eyes

602. Chichester: Multiple sightings of a black dog in a house in Westgate Street which was the scene of a murder when it was a pub

603. Ditchling: A story says that a black dog with no head used to haunt an area known as Black Dog Hill

604. West Hoathley: Tradition of a ghost dog known locally as Gytrack

SUTHERLAND

605. Craig'n Ordan: Legend of a large black dog with glowing eyes which emerged from the loch. It had a human face and horns, and spat sparks and fire

606. Kildonan: Legend of a black dog with two heads which guarded a pot of gold at the bottom of a stagnant pool

WARWICKSHIRE

607. Blacklow Hill: Reputed site of the execution of Piers Galveston by the Earl of Warwick, who was known as the Black Dog of Arden

608. Brewery Hill: A woman reports seeing a black dog which fades out and rises into the air

609. Little Compton: Tradition of a black dog at Pill Lane which is said to be the ghost of a woman called

Partington who killed herself

610. Coventry: A man sees a dog which he hits with his riding crop. The dog explodes

611. Coventry: A man sees a dog which seems to walk through a hedge and then disappear with a flash. A death occurs shortly afterwards

612. Coventry: 1949 – a man sees a large dog in a field

613. Meon Hill: A black dog was said to have been seen by a man shortly before his sister died. He saw it on multiple occasions and on the last it turned into a headless woman in a black dress

614. Mickleton: A black dog known as the Mickleton Hooter because of the noise that it makes. Associated with Meon Hill and hence may be connected with the previous entry

615. Radway: A large black dog is said to appear in front of people and then vanish in the area of Radway Grange

616. Snitterfield: Second World War – A large black dog was seen at Brook House and ran across the garden without leaving any footprints

617. Warwick Castle: Legend of a 15th century Earl accusing a dairy maid of witchcraft. She shut herself in a tower and when the door was broken down a black dog with red eyes was in her place

WESTMORLAND (See also Lake District)

618. Bela-side Hill: A headless black dog is said to walk between Beetham and Milnthorpe each night at midnight

619. Eggholme: The road between Burneside and Kendal is said to be haunted by a headless dog

620. Kell Bank Lane: Tradition of a goblin said to assume the form of a large mastiff dog. Known as the Kell Bank Dobby

621. Kirkby Stephen: A black dog is said to run nightly across the road on Stainmore

622. Lyth Valley: A ghost dog was seen by a witness at

Crossthwaite but there are no further details

623. Shap: A tradition of a ghost which takes the same form as the Kell Bank Dobby (see entry 620 above)

624. Shap: 1937 – multiple reports over successive nights of motorists on the A6 seeing a dog running in front of their car and then jumping over a stone wall which had a three hundred foot drop on the other side

WILTSHIRE

625. All Cannings: 1920s – a dog chases a man into the village

626. Black Dog Hill: A folk tale of two men (one of whom owns a dog) fighting over a farmer's daughter has given rise to a number of place names featuring the term Black Dog

627. Burbage: A man is accompanied by a dog which subsequently disappears

628. Burton Hill: A black dog is said to haunt the main road at Burton Hill between the milestone and the old coaching pool

629. Chippenham area: 1930s – a woman sees an apparition of a knight in armour with a black dog in a church but nobody else present sees anything

630. Collingbourne Kingston: A black dog is said to haunt the A346 / A338 from Marlborough

631. Collingbourne Woods: A murderer escaping from the police was said to go into the woods but be scared by a large black dog and come back out, whereupon he was captured

632. Cow Down: A large black dog was said to appear and frighten the local people who were holding a fete, to the extent that they did not hold one in the location again

633. Cricklade: Abingdon Court Lane is said to be haunted by a ghost dog

634. Cricklade: 1940s – a woman is very frightened by the sighting of a dog

635. Crockerton: A large black dog is traditionally said to

walk an unnamed road on certain nights, emitting fire from its nostrils

636. Devizes: A man walking on Quaker's Walk, reputed to be haunted by ghosts of Quakers, saw a black dog disappear through a hedge

637. Doghill Barrow: A prehistoric site near Stonehenge where the ghost of a black dog standing guard has been reported

638. Donhead St Mary: 1950s – report of a sighting of a dog by a male witness

639. Foxham: Approx. 1963 – A motorist sees a black dog pass in front of his car but not appear on the other side. Two weeks later he is rushed to hospital for a serious operation

640. Grafton: Two people are out walking. One of them sees a dog but the other can see nothing

641. Great Durnford: Late 19th century – a black dog was said to haunt the chalk pits between Durnford and Netton

642. Hilmarton: Something dragging a chain is reported to thrown a cyclist off of his bike

643. Horton: A man was accompanied by a black dog prior to a death

644. Inglesham: A black dog was said to haunt the area

645. Longleat: Vague reference to a sighting but no further details

646. Manton: 1910s – A woman sees an apparition of a dog with a chain in her house

647. Melksham: A man reports being chased by an animal which was described as either a dog or a bear

648. Moredon: An appearance of a large black dog which vanishes

649. Pewsey Vale: 1940s – two witnesses report seeing a lady in black accompanied by a dog

650. Pewsey Vale: 1990 – Two people out walking report seeing a dog which passes between them very silently

651. Quemerford: 1910s – a man sees a dog with a chain which appears to walk through a door

652. Ramsbury: A hears a dog with a chain but cannot see it

653. Sharcott: A girl going to Sunday School with her sister saw a black dog which sounded as though it had a chain

654. Sharcott: A man (related to the girl in entry 653 above but generations later) was followed by a black dog whilst riding his bike at night

655. South Wraxall: 1999 – A witness walking their dog sees a black dog but their own pet, who normally barks at other dogs, ignores it

656. South Wraxall: 1993 – a couple out walking see a black dog, like a mastiff, in front of them. When they reach the spot where it was standing after it has walked off towards the hedge there is no sign of it

657. Stert: 1971 – a couple in a cart see a dog pass them and then disappear

658. Stourton: The Sloane Track is said to be haunted by a headless horseman followed by a black dog

659. Stourton: A black dog is said to haunt a bricked up room at Brook House

660. Tedworth: Old records of a poltergeist case which sometimes took the form of a black dog

661. Tockenham: 1912 – a ten-year-old boy sees a dog with a chain

662. Warminster: Mid-1990s – two people driving at night see a large black animal cross the road in front of them on the bypass

663. Wilbury: A black dog and the ghost of a clergyman are said to be seen between Wilbury House and the lodge gates

664. Wilbury: A man walking along The Grove is accompanied by a black dog which leaves at the Double Shuttle

665. Wootton Bassett: A black dog was said to be seen on a piece of road which was known as Black Dog

666. Wootton Rivers: Deane Water Bottom is said to

be haunted by a black dog

667. Wootton Rivers: A woman out driving sees two dogs in the road

668. Wootton Rivers: A female witness walking her dog is passed by a large dog

WORCESTERSHIRE

669. Bewdley: 1943 – a man reports seeing a dog walk past him at an unspecified location

670. Bordesley Abbey: 1864 – Two men in a ruined abbey see a dog on two nights

671. Bredon: During World War II – A girl in bed in late afternoon sees a black dog with red eyes walk from the fireplace, circle the room and disappear by the door

672. Lulsley: A black dog has been seen here near old Storridge and Callow's Leap

WREXHAM

673. Bwlchgwny – A man who often walked at night was always accompanied by a black dog with a chain between here and Coedpoeth

YORKSHIRE

674. Almondbury: 1820 – a man is accompanied home by a dog

675. Almondbury: A man is accompanied home by a dog which turns into a calf

676. Almondbury: A man is accompanied by a dog

677. Arncliffe: A man is accompanied by a dog and the event foretells the death of a friend. A note states that this account may be fictitious

678. Barton Quarry: 1931 – A man cycling is passed by a whole pack of dogs but cannot touch them

679. Berwick: Tradition of a dog with a chain, referred to

as Padfoot, at the town gate

680. Billingham: 1999 – two people see a dog with glowing eyes on a number of occasions

681. Bradford: A man is accompanied by a dog at the same time that the owner of the local Hall is dying

682. Cowling: A black dog is said to haunt the road outside the village of Keighley. It is referred to as Bargoed or Baygoed

683. Darrington: An old woman is accompanied by a dog on numerous nights

684. Dinnington: A family hear a dog scratching at their door, but cannot see anything

685. East Riding: A white dog known as Willie Sled's Dog is said to haunt a crossroads at Brigham Lane

686. Fewston: 1600s – a family suffers a series of hauntings which include the apparition of a black dog

687. Grassington: A man walking down Mill Lane heard the sound of rattling chains and then saw a black dog

688. Greenhow Hill: A man reported seeing a dog on the road on many occasions

689. Holden Rag: An apparition said to be seen either as a black dog or as a piece of white cloth

690. Horbury: A man saw a white dog which sometimes walked on two legs. When trying to hit it, his stick passed straight through

691. Horbury: A ghost dog, referred to as Padfoot, was said to haunt a lane near Ossett

692. Horton: A black dog with horrid eyes was said to haunt many roads here

693. Hull: 1986 – various members of a family report seeing a "two-dimensional" dog which vanishes. A death occurs shortly afterwards

694. Ivelet: A black dog apparition here is said to precede a tragic event

695. Keighley 1893 – A dog is said to protect a man from robbers

696. Kettleness: 1920s – A fisherman sees a dog appear

and disappear on a number of occasions

697. Kettleness: 1950s – A man sees a dog which emerges from the sea

698. Kirkby Overblow: A phantom dog is said to haunt the area

699. Knight Stainforth Hall: Tradition of the ghosts of men and dogs being seen between the Hall and Dog Hill.

700. Leeming Bar: 2001 – Two women driving on the A684 see a black dog run in front of their car. It passes through the bonnet. A man they spoke to when they arrived at their destination reportedly killed himself later

701. Mosborough Hall: A couple see a dog which puts its head on their bed and then disappears

702. North Anston: 1993 – a man out climbing sees a dog

703. Oxwells: A spring between Wreghorn and Headingly Hill has a piece of waste land above it which is said to be haunted by a black dog

704. Pontefract: A woman is followed by a dog when returning from work at night

705. Sheffield: 1933 – A girl of eight sees a dog every night in her bedroom. It walks from the door and round the bed

706. Skipton: Tradition of a haunting by a dog referred to as the Guy-trash

707. Skirethornes: A man attacks a dog and is reportedly crushed to death

708. Swillington: A woman sees the apparition of a dog which rolls along and changes its shape

709. Throstlenest: A black dog is said to haunt a glen between Darlington and Houghton

710. Troller's Gill: Tradition of a black dog haunting this spot

711. Unknown location: 1930s – A woman walking at night is accompanied by a dog which protects her from unsavoury characters

712. Unknown location: A man sees a dog at a stile. He kicks it and it drags him home

713. Wakefield: Tradition of a haunting by a Barguest-type dog in various places

714. Wentworth: 1960s – a man out cycling sees a dog running next to him. It then reportedly runs straight through him

715. Wharfedale: An elderly man sees a dog. No further details

716. Wharfedale: A man is accompanied by a black dog which is said to open gates for him

717. Wreghorn: A child sees a pack of howling dogs being led by one with eyes like flames at the time that a local squire dies

718. Whitby: A man driving reports seeing a dog which fades away. It is sitting on a barrow

719. York: Tradition of a haunting by a black dog referred to as a Barguest

A Note on Further Reading

When working in the field of folklore research and recording a variety of primary and secondary sources must be considered: historic documents, journal articles, oral traditions, field recording and personal correspondence to name but a few.

With the nature of this work and research, it is impractical, if not impossible, to be able to provide a detailed bibliography for this book. Many of the sightings recorded were told in personal correspondence and have by necessity been made anonymous. Additionally, in working with the archives of other researchers, some references to written documents are found to only be partially recorded. Where accounts have been collected by researchers now deceased, it is impossible to be able to safely state whether permission for names to be published was obtained.

All the names of witnesses in this publication have been cited because permission to do so was given where these people have been in direct contact with the author. In other cases, relatives or descendants have given permission and in further cases information was clearly in the public domain.

Any bibliography would, therefore, be incomplete and of limited use. Where it is possible to do so, the author will be happy to supply further information on references, many of which have been made in-line in the body text of the book.

There have been few full studies of this subject to suggest as further reading. Cited within this book are some publications which contain useful information on the phenomenon and the author would encourage use of these cited titles as suggested further reading for a general overview. Additionally, some useful articles may be found in Folklore (the journal of the Folklore Society) and in the pages of Fortean Times magazine.

However, one of the most valuable resources for exploring this subject in more detail are the books on local folklore, legends and traditions which have been published in the past in every county of the United Kingdom, and in many other countries around the world. It is in these pages that many of these old stories will be found recorded. Many of these books have been out of print for some time but may be found in second hand bookshops. Additionally, public libraries and local history resource libraries are your friends in research such as this, as on those shelves many of these titles lie waiting to be discovered. This is a good place to continue your journey.

CPSIA information can be obtained
at www.ICGtesting.com
Printed in the USA
JSHW010139110220
4156JS00002B/29